The

Raising of

Money

The
Raising of
Money

35 Essentials

Trustees Are Using

to Make a Difference

Jim Lord

Published by
New Futures Press, Inc.
PO Box 66518
Seattle, WA 98166-0158
www.newfuturespress.com

ISBN 978-0-9799485-0-3
Manufactured in the United States of America

Dedication

To the Volunteer

THE VOLUNTEER—the advocate—is the heart and soul of philanthropy.

Working my way across the country as a consultant, I would often arrive in a community that was new to me. One thought always emerged: I would soon be meeting "the best people when they're at their best."

They would be the best—because they would be the most successful leaders. And they would be at their best—because they would be giving of their energies and resources in a voluntary spirit.

The result of their commitment would be to enrich the quality of people's lives—and, in fact, to advance our civilization.

There is no greater honor than to serve these people, these advocates. They are, indeed, "the best at their best."

Table of Contents

Preface

On Brevity

IN 1656, PASCAL WROTE to a friend: "I have only made this letter rather long because I have not had time to make it short."

That's still the way it is. It takes *more* time to make a communication short and to the point than it does to spill forth all our thoughts and ideas.

People resent the time they have to spend reading or listening for information. Most don't really read much at all; they skim.

When we communicate with people, as much thought deserves to go into what can be left out as what will be included.

In making a case to a prospective donor, for example, many organizations try to give the person every possible reason to contribute. This accomplishes two things:

1. It demonstrates a lack of confidence and clarity on the part of the organization.
2. It's *boring.* "The man with the unimpressive argument," as the saying goes, "rattles off many of them."

The only person who's really interested in reading or listening to a long-winded monologue is the person who writes or delivers it.

—*◊◊◊*—

So in writing this book, we've tried to take the time to make it short.

We hope that when you lay it down, you'll feel that the words of Winston Churchill might, in some measure, apply:

"Out of intense complexities, intense simplicities emerge."

Introduction to
the Second Edition

*Now is the best time to take a peek at this book ...
and to raise money*

It's hard to believe how the world has taken such a turn or two, in such a brief span.

Yes, we are in the midst of the most profound economic situation you and I have ever seen. At the same time, if you look for them, there are encouraging signs of a renewed pulse of civic engagement, a new dialogue.

What a time to talk of raising money.

To fuel ourselves in these unusual days, we just might want to turn our attention to the hope (yes, the *hope*) our organizations represent.

Hope—confidence in the future—is a prerequisite for major philanthropy. Indeed, without a belief that a difference can be made in the world, that the future can be shaped by our efforts today, why would anyone give of themselves?

The way I see it, the very existence of our "organizations of social good" can embolden all of us. After all, the voluntary choice to create and sustain these institutions and agencies reflects the very best of who we are as human beings. And our accomplishments through these organizations show us glimpses of what can be possible.

Your investing yourself in this cause is every bit as much a reason for people around you to be encouraged about the future. For your spirit of contribution shines all the brighter in what might otherwise seem to be dim days.

So, in support of our navigating today's turbulent waters, I offer this thin volume as a chance to think together about a new, confident conversation. A conversation of consequence.

My intent is to offer a solid footing for creating the world we want. How? By looking back at the "old-fashioned" principles of civic engagement and philanthropic spirit that were described in the first edition of this book, a generation ago. And by seeing which of these fundamentals have endured long enough (and through enough ups, downs and sideways) to qualify as timeless tenets.

To amplify those enduring ideas, I bring to you my fresh study of hope and promise. (Yes, you actually can study such things.) That's the purpose of this new introduction and the afterword that concludes this new edition.

Hope, choice and you

WHEN I SPEAK of hope, I mean a force in a person and among people that is beyond mere optimism or a "positive" outlook.

My kind of hope is *grounded*, always rooted in recognizing past and present strengths, resources and capabilities. (At the same time, it may also be spirited, as "faith in the future" suggests.)

Such a stance is especially important now, as we see an unprecedented longing for leadership that is both inspired and inspiring.

If being inspired and inspiring others is what you want, then it's worth asking: What can fortify hope more than seeing significant voluntary acts on the civic stage? Such actions, and the spirit of those behind them, will give most of us a real shot in the arm.

So what I'm saying is that hope is at once a precondition of great deeds and a result. A virtuous circle if ever I saw one.

Nearly as much of a prerequisite to success is feeling that one has choices, and that's exactly what we have. Philanthropy *is* choice and freedom.

After all, our causes give people ways to do what they want to do, where they want to do it, and how they want to do it. Next to the ballot box, philanthropy is the clearest expression of a choiceful democracy.

When it's expected and assumed, when it is approached as either tax or entitlement, the spirit of philanthropy is compromised.

So stay at the center of the ideals we call freedom and democracy—the core of free societies—and treat philanthropy as a voluntary expression of a person's desires and identity.

It deserves repeating: Hope is both a condition of philanthropy and a result. It works both ways. Once hope has kindled philanthropy, then confidence, freedom, choice, personal initiative, and democracy are all advanced.

Where else in our lives than the civic stage do we get a better opportunity to declare what we believe in? And invite others to join us?

That's why you will find here a reservoir of an encouraging and confident spirit.

This book was written to reinforce you, the volunteer leader, as a voice for positive expectations and possibility, especially in this season. If any days call for you and me to take a stand for hope and confidence and for vibrant philanthropy, it is today.

So I want to see your voice, your presence, your personal power amplified as an *advocate for hope, choice and personal initiative.* Indeed, I've taken it as my life's work to strengthen this force in good folks like you.

But first: Why I'm glad I went into hiding

MORE THAN 25 YEARS ago, I put together *The Raising of Money* as an "executive summary" of the proven principles and practices of raising large money (and doing so with respect).

At the time, I was consulting for a national firm on capital campaigns, often seen as the pinnacle of fundraising practice, where the stakes are highest and the people the most influential. (In just the four years before I began to write *The Raising*, my service took me into living temporarily in a sequence of 28 cities.)

Working in this field gave me such an education. It taught me about human behavior, about how people become inspired to do things they thought were beyond reach. Those experiences profoundly affected me. I wonder how else, where else I could have learned what I have.

Even early on, I sought to put the raising of money into a much larger context of personal initiative. That's allowed me to see the noble and profound nature of this endeavor. (You'll be taking advantage of this experience and mindset as you turn these pages.)

Then about 15 years ago, I widened my view: to take on the whole system—an organization, cause, or community—and also the desires of individuals to create the society they wanted. I found that "fundraising" was vastly more effective when seen in that framework.

Eager to find better ways to do this larger work, I dug into an extensive learning program, studying with global thought leaders the most advanced ideas in social psychology and organization development, even community development and global social change. Always looking for what I could learn about what gets people riled up and moving, motivated to work for what they believed in.

And for more than a decade, I stayed away from conferences and invitations to speak, and met only with those who came to my private, by-invitation workshops. Hundreds of people participated in those programs, from more than 50 countries. What an experience.

Along with me, they conducted thousands of interviews to uncover the conditions that are behind people stepping forward and investing themselves in the future. (Isn't that what philanthropy is, when at its best?)

Retreating pays big dividends

I WAS SEARCHING for the "secret" to the largest success— how we can best bring our ideals to life. Well, that might sound like hype, or at least it does to me. But that's what I was looking for: the "secret power" that could unlock a whole new level of possibility.

A curious thing happened along the way.

More and more, I found myself working directly with civic leaders, and with the philanthropicallyinclined ("donors"), to support them in what they wanted to do, creating the kind of world *they* wanted to see.

You might think I was searching for ways to achieve optimal fundraising performance. But in a way it was the opposite: In the intimate setting of private programs, I was *inside* the experience of civic leaders and donors, walking with them ... even laying the roadbed for them and with them ... so they could exercise their ideals and create a new tomorrow.

Well, perhaps that actually *is* the key to extraordinary results in the raising of money—understanding, at a deep and personal level, what those folks are about, what they're thinking, what they care about, what they want. Oh yes, and the strengths they have to get there, whether they're aware of them or not.

All along, I kept intending to re-release *The Raising of Money*. In fact, I have a new book for donors that I held off on releasing, so I could first re-issue the one in your hands. Raising money is that important to these times.

It's a good thing I gave *The Raising* a rest, for I've returned to it with this much wider view, new insights, and, well, wisdom. (It's cool to be getting older.)

So here you have it, now for your use are the 35 key ideas that appeared in the original edition of this book and have, I'm told, become even more relevant in the years since. I've liked hearing that, as you can imagine.

But first, what's new, what would I change? What could affect your role in making policy and fostering a culture that will sustain great philanthropy?

The first essential

IN THE ORIGINAL EDITION, I preached as forcefully as I could to let go of the whole notion of "needs." In fact, I made that idea the first essential. Every speech I gave in those days began with the admonition that "organizations have no needs." That's as true today as it was back then.

In recent years I've asked more and more insistently: Instead of focusing on needs, what about appreciating our resources, assets, and strengths, whether organizational or personal?

Could that give us more energy to realize our aspirations?

For many, this is a cultural change, which calls for creating new habits or remembering old ones. I've found that it takes purposeful, consistent voice and reminders on a group and a personal level—even a degree of discipline—for an organization to move, or keep moving, in this direction.

Any effort is more than worth it. Your cause becomes a more compelling investment when you shift people's attention from what most of us think of as the needs that the world presents ... to the resources that are also all around us, if only we can see them.

It bears repeating this idea; it is that vital: The very existence of your organization—and your presence as a volunteer leader—is a reason for people to have confidence in the future.

Right now is the best time in our lifetimes to encourage this hope, to promote confident conversations, to enliven civic discourse. And then to watch what happens.

And yes, if you and your cause can shine brightly—especially when so many see dim days—you *will* attract people. Plenty of people are eager to lift their gaze from problems to potentials.

They'll come with their strengths and resources more present. What they will do with those resources may surprise you.

They'll put their money where they see promise.

After all, a force is present, waiting to be activated ...

People want to give, so help them give

PEOPLE *WANT* TO GIVE.

Embracing this fundamental truth makes the work of inviting investment so much easier (and an entirely different proposition than "fundraising" from the reluctant).

I wish I had said it plainly and boldly 25 years ago.

Here's what made it so vivid to me: Some years ago, I created a tiny private seminar for a few folks who were in my inner circle of workshop alums. I invited behavioral psychologist Dr. Aryeh Nesher to come from New York City to teach us what we could apply to

philanthropy from what he'd learned from selling dia-
monds and Ferraris. He began by telling us:

> In business, we say, "A customer wants to buy,
> but he doesn't want to be sold. So help him buy."
> In fundraising we can say, "A donor wants to
> give, but he doesn't want to be solicited. So help
> him give."

It's so obvious, once stated. But it changes everything, doesn't it?

I've come to believe that this assumption—that
people want to give—is fundamental to all 35 essentials
in this book. The idea so imbues every page that I took
it for granted.

Our first job is to realize this truth, rather than
think we have to convince anyone against their will.

In fact, the point is quite the opposite. We want to
strengthen their will, their sense of personal power and
efficacy. That's what will move them from wanting to
give to actually doing so.

Whether in casual conversation when you happen
to run into someone, or in a scheduled meeting, it's
useful to carry with you this basic idea. If all you do is
shift the monologue in your mind, you've gone a long
way to treating the person differently.

Better yet, when you reframe the dialogue based
on knowing that people want to give, that perspective
spreads informally and organically, one conversation
at a time.

You'll find people will want to be around you when
you recognize them as the "contributing members of

society" they are, and when you see more of what we have going for us.

This sense automatically elevates the conversation to one of greater promise. You can claim this higher ground because of your association with this organization of social good. It gives you the right to speak of optimism and confidence.

After all, you're merely reinforcing and legitimizing the desire to give that's already there, even if it was faint before you stepped in and turned up the volume.

But what about the person who seems to not want to give? I'd bet it's at least partly because of how they've been asked before. The way a person is pursued can leave them feeling like prey.

By contrast, you and your organization can set the stage so that their giving will be more of a collaboration with you, one that brings them deep satisfaction, meaning and even joy.

Imagine that.

When we meet with them—as long as they're doing most of the talking and we're seeking to learn where they're coming from and to gain the benefit of their experience—we will attract them.

Indeed, we draw people closer whenever we slow down enough to let our natural, authentic curiosity come to the surface.

The ideal relationship is based on an interest you share, a desire to contribute to the community, maybe even seeing the possibilities of what you can do together.

As many folks say, "It's the personal relationship."

In this way, you show that you value the donor—the person—more than the donation.

I'd like to get a little more specific with you.

The power of example

MANY PEOPLE THINK they have to know a lot of details about an organization before going to visit someone. It's fine when someone is so well-prepared, if it bolsters their confidence.

On the other hand, it seems to me that most people overdo this "product knowledge." When someone asks a question, it's easy enough to get answers. Yet many of us assume before we walk in the door that we should know the organization as well as a salesperson knows a product line.

This can be so daunting a task that many volunteers are dissuaded from ever becoming involved in development.

Let's make this easier: A volunteer has something so much more valuable than knowledge of the organization. What they have is their belief in the cause: why they care about the organization and why they give of themselves. That is what will come across most vividly.

That personal *why* trumps a recitation of the facts every time.

This may sound as if I'm suggesting we enter into

a "me" conversation. Rather, we're merely opening the door to person-to-person connecting, moving the visit from an official *institutional* presentation to a more *personal* conversation, based on shared interests.

It is often said that one who is making a visit can walk in the door feeling calm and confident if they kick themselves out of the way and let the cause walk in first.

While that can be a useful tactic, I want to make sure we keep mindful of our own experiences and what it is that attracts us to give of ourselves.

So to prepare, I suggest people simply answer a few questions for themselves: Why do you care about this cause? Why do you serve? Why have you given? (One answer may cover all three questions.)

When you know for yourself what moves you—even if you speak little of it—you will show up in a different way. You'll have a forceful wind at your back and solid grounding under your feet.

That is what I meant earlier when I brought up the secret to your success, your secret power.

To a large degree that presence comes from your being connected to an idea larger than yourself. Just as you've identified with the ideals of the cause and are associated with the works of the organization, you're offering that to another. Being connected with like-minded people can be one of the most significant aspects of a person's life.

Let me try to impress upon you the power you have because of the role you hold ...

The volunteer is still the key

THE PROFESSION THAT manages the raising of money has become more and more sophisticated, with professional certifications, even academic degrees and research. It's also become more professionalized, in the number of staff and their capabilities.

Moreover, professionals are much more at the center of the visit with the donor than they were just a couple of decades ago.

On that point, I take a contrarian stance.

You've probably figured it out from what I've already said, but this bears a strong statement: I want to see volunteers exhibiting their leadership role by visiting with folks.

(The professional staff you work with may see things differently. Trust their judgment. They know more than I do about your particular situation.)

You may think that bringing volunteers into the center is done to ease the work of staff or save money. Quite the contrary. In fact, it can be more work for the staff, even introducing some complexity into their jobs.

Here's a case in point: As a major university readied itself for a $3 billion campaign, one of the most senior and successful development officers walked up to me after a workshop and confided, "The University's plan for us to work with volunteers—it has me worried, well even scared a bit. I know how to do my job. I've been very successful, but I have no idea what will happen if I have to work with volunteers."

The reason it's worth this professional going to the effort of working with volunteers is because philanthropy is at its core *voluntarism*.

This is a theme worth returning to again and again: Philanthropy is choice. The voluntary spirit nourishes vibrant philanthropy.

Volunteers are more effective, to boot, in contrast to what some may tell you.

Here's why: The sheer presence of a volunteer—one who shows evidence of having invested themselves in the cause—makes the most compelling and persuasive statement.

By simple fact of their showing up, even before a word is spoken. That's what I'm talking about.

If this volunteer knows that their commitment is "full-of-meaning," even if only to themselves, their presence will influence the person being called upon. If this volunteer speaks of the commitment and what it means to them, that will carry even more force, more than the most elaborate presentation or the most ingenious solicitation strategies and techniques.

This exemplary commitment serves to encourage by example, rather than by advice. (It can even influence the organization's staff to see the worth of the cause in a whole new light, and the importance of their own work.)

What I've written here may fly in the face of assumptions your board may have made, if you thought you were hiring a development staff as if they were a sales force, to get out there and sell. (Perhaps so you wouldn't have to do it yourselves.) But such a strategy takes the heart, and much of the effectiveness, out of the raising of money for your cause.

If voluntarism is at the heart of philanthropy, there's more to this than the dollars, a lot more ...

The donor's quest

THE SENSE OF VALIDATION and potency that the donor derives from the act of philanthropy may be even more important than its visible results. That is, more powerful than the services the money provides.

A bold claim, don't you think?

Yes, I believe this whole ball game is about just how much a person can come to believe in their personal strength and efficacy. I believe that so strongly, in fact, that you'll find me suggesting on the opening page of my next book ...

Imagine if everyone who wanted to change the world *knew* they could.

It doesn't even matter if they change it. I'm serious. Just believing in their power to influence the world—to make a difference—will change the world because they will *be* different. They will think, look, act differently. They will be more of who they are.

This is what I mean: When a person feels they have agency, power, efficacy, their little corner of the world changes, it becomes enlivened, ennobled. The people around this person are influenced. The kind of force for good I'm talking about is an antidote to powerlessness, helplessness and a depressed, pessimistic sense of the future.

And the world changes as it experiences this example.

I know that I'd be gratified to live in a world where more people believe that a difference can be made, and that they themselves can and do make a difference.

That's my desired world.

I've seen it, and it's one of the most exalted and inspiring experiences of the human spirit.

And our own quest

As DICK BUTTERFIELD, a visionary civic leader in Bermuda, put it in a note to me before a workshop, "I can easily propose and advocate ideas, but the other person may be less than persuaded or motivated. I want to learn how to help—or is it 'allow'—other people to surface aspirations that they are keen to carry forward."

Indeed!

He—and you—make the donor's quest possible. You have the great honor of giving people a way to make a difference of heroic proportions.

People already want to give. It's up to us to *allow* them.

Your Quest

I AM CONVINCED that far more idealistic
aspiration exists than is ever evident.
Just as the rivers we see are much less
numerous than the underground streams,
so the idealism that is visible is minor
compared to what men and women carry
in their hearts, unreleased or scarcely
released. Mankind is waiting and longing
for those who can accomplish the task of
untying what is knotted and bringing the
underground waters to the surface.

—*Albert Schweitzer*

What else would I change?

MUCH TO MY SURPRISE, I'm being told that nearly all of *The Raising of Money* has stood the test of time. It's a bit of a shock. After all, it's been more than 25 years since it was first published. (The initial release of the book was so long ago that a typesetter provided galleys that were *literally* cut and pasted!)

Of course, I could write here about recent changes with the Internet, strategic planning, the roles of consultants, feasibility studies, marketing, and many other topics (which I do in my resources for professionals). But here, I want to keep the focus on the fundamentals of human behavior that are most important to board members.

And because the focus is on major philanthropy, I've made an assumption that the most effective means will be used: face-to-face visits, and especially organized in a campaign.

Little did I know the book would be so durable when I chose to focus on such behavioral *principles*—how people tend to behave when they invest themselves—instead of the *techniques* of fundraising.

You've just read in the first few pages what I felt called for a rethink. Your having that introduction and an afterword at the back of the book allows the original pages to be left nearly as they were first published.

Only a few items have been altered in the manuscript for readability. Here they are, in case you're curious.

Where have all the prospects gone?

I used to call them "prospects," and improved it to "prospective donors." Then I began to simply respect people as "donors"—because essentially everyone contributes somewhere, right? (So let's make it a part of their identify and give them the credit they deserve.)

And now? I've come to often call these good folks simply "people."

I've also shifted my thinking from cultivating a *person* to cultivating a *relationship* with a person or cultivating their *interest* in something. Treating people less like objects, and more like colleagues and friends.

By the way, if you're still "cultivating prospects," let me say it's often easiest to use the words everyone else uses. Remember, it's taken me 40 years to make the shift. And I think about these things all the time for you.

What do pronouns have to do with raising money?

You'll notice other important changes in language. This one on pronouns is even of historical import. Language is that significant? Yes, the words we choose have everything to do with how we think, how we talk, and what's possible.

When the book was first released in 1983 we used the "he or she" form. Now, as English teachers and editors cringe, usage is changing again to where a writer can refer to "he or she" as "them." (It's amazing to recall that when I entered this field, it was seen as the domain of men. The extent of a woman's influence was thought to be "pillow talk." And professionally, there were only male campaign directors. Now in Spring 2009, one study reports more women than men are leading in making philanthropic decisions in U.S. households.)

Can we drop the *needs*?

As I've said more than once, it's time to let go of the notion of "needs." The first and easiest step is to remove that word from our vocabulary.

Starting with needs gives us a diminished view of the future. Just enough to get by, rather than the world we most desire … it shrinks the dream, drains the energy and sets us up for burn-out.

Little here to attract and excite significant philanthropy.

So where do you start instead? You shift the focal point—and the conversation—from needs to what the organization and cause has going for it.

Sounds easy enough, but I must admit that *needs, necessity* and *problems* are so much a part of the language of our lives. They're often assumed to be the only reason to do something (rather than to act out of the desire to shape the world we want, or because it's just part of our identity). Given my aversion to the idea of being needy, it surprised me to see that even I had written at many points in this book that "you *need* to do this" or "you *should* do that."

In this new edition, I changed many of those instances and similar ones in the interest of making your read easier. I even changed the book's original subtitle to eliminate the "should."

Introduction to
the Original Edition

THIS IS A BOOK about *people*—how they feel, how they think and act, and what happens between them when they're engaged in the enterprise of philanthropy.

The intent of this small volume is to report what we've come to understand about this phenomenon. On these pages can be found the most important principles of raising money—no more, and no less. At least, that is our intention.

We have not attempted to cover every facet of philanthropy, every fund-raising technique. The focus is on the art and science of significant philanthropy—*giving* that is advanced by a personal visit and often structured in a campaign. The reasons will become apparent.

This book reflects an increasingly specific approach to the raising of funds. It's an approach that asks us to be more intentional, more organized and more strategic than we used to be. The focus is less on getting donations per se, and more on the development of donors and the development of organizations.

This is not a "how-to" manual on fund raising. In the day-to-day practice of philanthropy, most decisions are "judgment calls" that depend on circumstance and opportunity. This book will serve only as a backdrop against which this drama is played out.

In the final analysis, raising money is a *personal* business. Results will come from people, not from books. As Shakespeare said, "Action is eloquence."

The

Raising of

Money

I

Working from
the Perspective of
the Donor

The days of hand-wringing and

arm-twisting are drawing to a close.

Today, the successful organization

invites people to invest in

an enterprise's strengths.

1

Organizations Have No Needs

TRYING TO RAISE MONEY on the basis of an organization's needs will work just about as well as trying to obtain a bank loan by pleading poverty. Panhandling is as ineffective with donors as it is with bankers.

Many organizations believe that the more compelling their needs and the more desperate for funds they appear, the more successful at fund-raising they'll be.

But donors are tired of hearing these pleas over and over again. In fact, from the viewpoint of the donor, an organization *has no needs*.

The organization has strengths and capabilities. It's most successful when showing itself as poised to capitalize on these potentials.

Of course a community, indeed society, may have problems. People may have needs. But organizations, institutions and agencies are reservoirs of assets and possibilities. One urban university translated this attitude into words when it described itself as "an instrument for the advancement of society."

(Read between the lines here in 2009, and you can discern the next level of understanding: even people and communities can be seen as bundles of resources, assets and strengths, yes, even those that appear most needy. Organizations are the vehicles for *organizing* this talent and these potentials.)

Other organizations still behave as if their own sense of lack is more their reality and more inspiring than their strengths and the power of those strengths to make a difference on behalf of donors. What Napoleon said more than 150 years ago can still be applied to them:

"Men take only their needs into consideration, never their abilities."

2

Seek Investment, Not Charity

INVITE YOUR PROSPECTIVE DONOR to make a wise investment that will produce benefits. Donors are tired of giving handouts to the needy.

John D. Rockefeller, Jr. said it well: "Never think you need to apologize for asking someone to give to a worthy object, any more than as though you were giving him an opportunity to participate in a high-grade investment."

For some reason, those of us involved in philanthropy used to think we were in the generosity business.

We operated on the premise that our organizations were entitled to charity—like the beggar who stationed himself every day near the office of a wealthy business-man. The beggar had received a dime a day from the man over a long period of time.

The businessman went out of town for a month. When he returned, he passed the beggar, who said to him with a slight tone of reproach, "You owe me three dollars."

———

Organizations are not entitled to charity. The days of hand-wringing and arm-twisting are drawing to a close.

The organizations that will prosper will be those that earn and attract *investment*. The ones that are advancing today are the ones in which people choose to invest.

The fact is that people give in order to *get*. They don't want to feel that they are "giving away" their money. They want to feel that they are investing it, and getting some-thing in return. (Often that something is to have the sense that they've made a difference among people.)

The Boys Clubs of America, for example, works with young people to build self-respect and self-reliance, and to combat crime and delinquency. Its theme is: "If we can help them now, then they can help us later."

The clubs invite donors to invest in solid, produc-tive citizens. It doesn't ask them to fund a deficit.

In the raising of funds—as in the providing of services—the key words are *achievement, accomplishment, performance* and *success.*

One of the nation's leading resident theatres used to appeal for funds on the basis of its own internal needs. The theatre felt it could count on the traditional generosity of the city's theatre lovers to "keep the doors open."

Then the institution realized that if it was ever going to expand its constituency beyond this family of insiders, it would have to present itself differently. The theatre began to look at the priorities of community leaders and to consider which ones the institution was in a position to help achieve.

Leading individuals and businesses in the city were concerned with building civic pride and improving the city's image nationally and internationally. As it happened, the theatre's facilities were located in the central city, and had been for more than 80 years. And not only did the theatre enjoy an international reputation; its name also incorporated the name of the city.

Therefore, a new fund-raising strategy was adopted. For the first time in years, the theatre didn't plead for help in order to avoid a deficit. Instead, it presented itself as a community asset that carried the city's name worldwide. The theatre portrayed itself as an enterprise in which those who cared about the city could invest.

The new strategy was successful. One of the results was that the theatre was able to complete its season without conducting its usual "spring beg" (as the volunteers used to call it). Another was that leading citizens who had never been theatre lovers became enthusiastic donors and volunteers.

This theatre adopted the marketplace perspective. It realized that the center of its universe is not the organization, but the *community*—the donor community. It realized that the interests and aspirations of the *donor* come first.

This transition from begging to marketing is one of the most profound changes in raising funds in recent years. Unfortunately, this new reality has yet to dawn on most organizations, which continue to maintain an inwardly focused and myopic point of view.

We don't have to be greedy. Money, it's said, flows in a stream. Having to "go to the well," as if there's only so much, is a mistaken notion. There's really quite enough money to be had—if only we're smart about it.

3

Position Your Cause in People's Minds

THE MOST ATTRACTIVE ORGANIZATIONS stand out from the crowd. They're the ones that know how to distinguish themselves as investment opportunities.

The attractive organization has adopted a stance that sets it apart from the many other things that compete for the attention of donors and volunteers.

How is this done? Using a method developed by business, the organization *positions* itself in the philanthropic marketplace. The key is to answer the question: What does the organization do well—or what *can* it do well—that matters to the community?

A museum, for example, does not compete for attention only with other museums. In the eyes of the donor, it also competes with colleges, performing arts groups, and even hospitals and social service agencies.

The competition is even broader than that. The museum, and every other organization, also competes for attention with the family, religion and work—the things that most folks put first.

So in positioning an organization, we want to understand what's on our prospective donor's mind— and to align our program with the person's established interests and priorities.

We want to think marketing, not selling. If we're offering something the person *already wants*, the "sale" comes naturally.

It's said, for example, that Black & Decker manufactures drills, but its customers buy holes. Charles Revson, founder of Revlon, said, "In the factory, we make cosmetics. In the stores, we sell hope."

An example: One major research university, located in a northern industrial state, was preparing for a capital campaign. At the same time, the state's leadership was trying to encourage high-technology industries and diversify the economy.

The university emphasized that it could help the state accomplish this goal by joining with business in research and development ventures.

This institution had identified its *distinctive competency*—the major benefit it was in a position to provide better than anyone else. An investment in the university would be an investment in high-tech prosperity.

———

A campaign slogan is often used to position the enterprise in the minds of its constituents. It serves as a constant reminder of the major benefit—what the campaign is all about.

One small and relatively unknown Midwestern college adopted as its campaign theme "The First Generation Campaign." This phrase emphasized the College's specialty: its expertise in educating first-generation college students.

This was a service that mattered to the leaders in the city where the college was located. It struck them as a worthwhile investment.

The college surprised many observers by attracting the city's top leadership to its campaign organization. The success of the campaign could be attributed, in no small measure, to shrewd positioning.

By aligning itself with the values and priorities of the leaders, this college distinguished itself from dozens of "good little colleges" that were seeking the support of the same people.

Many of these schools continue to struggle for survival—because they haven't succeeded in convincing anyone but their own faculty and alumni that they have a special role to play. Without a distinctive stance in the community, they face an uphill battle.

4

Listen to the Community

"I've got to follow them; I am their leader."
—*Alexandre Ledru-Rollin*

IF YOU WANT TO BE A PART of an organization advancing, the first step is really quite simple: Stop focusing on internal issues long enough to get outside the organization—and ask people what they think of it, the strengths they see, and what they want from it.

It's essential to listen to the donor community. If we can find out what's on *their* minds and where *they're* going, we'll be in a strong position to shape our offering accordingly.

If we're not tuned in to what the community is saying, we can easily get in trouble—for we may end up trying to coerce people. We may find ourselves trying to convince people how they *should* think and what they *should* do.

It's much easier to relate our program to what people already want.

For example, the public television and radio facility in a major Southern city recently had to raise a lot of money to upgrade its technical equipment. The organization realized that on its face, this was a drab and uninspiring proposition for the donor.

But this organization kept its ear to the ground. It knew that the city harbored a certain "inferiority complex" that its leaders badly wanted to overcome. So the station proposed to do something about it.

Better equipment, the station explained, would mean *better programs* about the city. Better programs would mean that people would *feel better* about their city. And if the programs were good enough, they might get national attention, helping to improve the city's image everywhere.

This group of people listened to its constituents, and it shaped its offering to harmonize with their interests. As a result, it raised more than anyone had ever expected.

Any organization is more likely to succeed in raising funds if it's really listening to the community—to the people who have the capacity to *bring about* success.

5

Listen to What Each
Donor Has to Say

THE "DONOR COMMUNITY" isn't an abstraction. It's made up of flesh-and-blood *people* with their own personal attitudes and preferences. Some of these people can turn an organization's dreams into realities—but only if we listen to them as individuals, find out what they want, and make our approach accordingly.

After all, it's been proven that the success of any program will, in the end, be determined by a very few people. Each of these, as one seasoned development professional observes, "is a campaign unto itself."

If a prospective donor is interested in cancer research, for example, it makes little sense to try to convince that person that they *should* contribute to a pediatric wing (no matter how much the institution "needs" one).

Our time will be better spent in hearing the person. We want to give people an opportunity to tell us their vision of what could be. Only then can we design an appropriate response.

"When I'm getting ready to reason with a man," said Abraham Lincoln, "I spend one-third of my time thinking about myself and what I am going to say, and two-thirds thinking about him and what he is going to say."

A little imagination and creativity can go a long way in "making the match" between person and program.

A major zoo was looking for a way to get a certain corporate leader interested in its program. Zoos had never been especially high on his list of priorities. He was an entrepreneur who was known for investing in education, and in projects that promoted free-enterprise values.

Realizing this, the organization didn't attempt to interest this individual in its capital construction program. Instead, the zoo proposed that he invest in its education department—which was distinguished by a special approach.

This zoo taught young people about human society by showing them how "animal societies" worked. The basic principles of competition, cooperation, adaptation and survival were related to the children's own future in a free society. This program provided the entrepreneur with an unusual opportunity to invest in the values that were most important to him.

Certainly, the interests of the donor community as a whole are important. So are the wants and desires of the organization's users—its students, visitors, clients, patrons or patients.

But when we want to influence a particular *individual,* what counts is that person's own thoughts and aspirations. Rather than making the same case to everyone, we want to listen and respond on a *personal* level.

Benjamin Franklin, not surprisingly, had some choice advice for us: "If you would persuade, you must appeal to interest, rather than the intellect."

6

Donors Will Tell You What They Want

HOW DO YOU FIND OUT WHAT'S going on in a person's mind? Psychologist George Kelly suggested, "Ask him; he may tell you."

Kelly's observation, obvious though it may seem, tends to escape us all from time to time. As the development of organizations becomes a more sophisticated "science," we devote considerable energy and resources to prospect research. We compile data on donors from every available source, except the donor.

The donor is the best source of all. We sometimes forget that most people like to be sought out for their opinions. A single face-to-face interview can be worth more than volumes of research. And we can learn quite a lot by developing the habit of attentive listening in the course of our daily activities.

Besides casual conversation, what other ways are there to find out what people want?

We'll go into more detail later, but in the raising of money, there are at least three:

1. Use mail or telephone surveys (but making the time for in-person visits is much better).
2. Create opportunities for dialogue with community leaders about your institution and its plans. One avenue is the "leadership awareness program."

3. Conduct a series of confidential, one-on-one interviews with community leaders—a feasibility study.

The point is that simply putting the right questions to a few of the right people can generate a wealth of valuable insights.

Here's an example of what can happen through a structured listening process.

One major university was contemplating a huge capital campaign that incorporated a number of programs. The personal priority of the university president was a new art gallery. Most of the "insiders" felt that a new cancer hospital would be most attractive to donors.

To find out what would work, the university conducted a series of interviews with some of its key donors. Surprise! The art gallery and cancer hospital were well received—but most people felt it would be best if the highest priority were to strengthen the already strong faculty.

What's more, the donors had their own ideas about which departments they'd like to see developed. The university had provided its own list of faculty chairs to be endowed. These met with a cool response.

This university understood that it wouldn't be a good idea to make its plans in a vacuum, or to guess what people *might* think of its ideas. This institution was sharp enough to ask—early enough so that its plans could be shaped accordingly.

Of course, there are values and other motivations

that run deeper than current interests. Why *do* people give? It's a fascinating study.

In his book, *Designs for Fund-Raising*, Harold J. "Si" Seymour postulated that people aspire simply "to be sought." Seymour also cited a study by Dr. Dorothea Leighton, an anthropologist, who concluded that each of us needs to feel we are "a worthwhile member of a worthwhile group."

Many people who have been doing this work for a long time feel that the key motivating factor is self-image. We all strive to bring our behavior into line with the way we think of ourselves. ("This is the kind of person I am.")

———

Understanding what people want is vital to the practice of raising money. We're in conversations with them, rather than assuming that we *already* know.

I'm reminded of an experience the reader has undoubtedly shared with me. You're in a restaurant, you've finished your cheeseburger, and you ask the waiter. "What can you offer for dessert?"

The waiter replies, "We only have apple pie today."

Little did he know that until that moment, at least, apple pie was exactly what you wanted. The poor fellow could see things only from his own viewpoint. He presumed to know what his "prospect" *didn't* want. We never know what a person wants—until we ask.

7

Make Your Case Larger Than the Organization

THE EFFECTIVE CASE FOR SUPPORT is like an investment prospectus for a business. It is designed to attract donors—who are, after all, investors.

The case is also like a good speech or the closing remarks of an attorney. It is designed to move people both intellectually and emotionally.

When we write a case for donors, we want it to touch them where they live and breathe. We want them to feel that investing in the program will make life better for them, for their children and grandchildren. We want them to feel that the community and the nation will be strengthened—even that *civilization itself* will be advanced by what they do.

The best casemakers have found that in order to move people on this level, it takes making your case *larger than the organization.* It's not enough to "tell the story" of the organization, to recite its history. It's equally ineffective to try to convince the person that the organization needs the money to avoid deterioration or collapse. (You already know that.)

What works best is to present a vision of the future— one that people find attractive, achievable and worth working for. The case demonstrates how the organization can make a special contribution to building that future. We want people to be *inspired* to play a part in making it happen. We want them to feel that they have a chance to make history—and that the time for action is now.

The best cases can be summed up in a few powerful sentences, or even a single memorable phrase. This kind of case is easy for volunteers to internalize, and to articulate to their prospective donors. The case doesn't attempt to "cover the waterfront" by including every conceivable reason to support the program.

—*∽∽*—

To bring the vision into focus, the case is expected to include the facts and logic, the data and the dollars to support the argument. Certainly, people want to know how many National Merit scholars the school is producing.

Donors are interested in your distinctive, innovative programs—your success stories. Give them examples, illustrations, case histories. But don't drown them in data. All the "vital statistics" belong somewhere else; the case itself is best when simple and brief. In a word, interesting.

The effective case also gives evidence of the *planning* behind the program. It shows prospective donors that the organization is well managed and strategic. And it explains how their investments will be applied in a timely fashion to the areas where they will produce the best results, the greatest benefits.

This kind of case is psychologically based in the donor's world, rather than developed from an internal, institutional perspective.

This may surprise you: Experience has shown that the strongest arguments come from those who will give and work for the cause, especially board members—from their deepest desires and highest aspirations. It makes sense to involve them in developing the case, not just approving it.

In other words, we take our cues from the people who can make the program a success. We interview them and even quote them in the case. When this is done, the case often turns out to be more useful before it's finished.

One Midwestern college, for example, was developing its case for an upcoming capital campaign. A certain trustee, a successful businessman, was interviewed for his thinking.

This philanthropist had previously endowed a center for free-enterprise education at the college. He chose this particular school because it openly advocated our nation's free social, political and economic institutions.

The resulting case positioned the college as an unusual investment opportunity for those who wanted to advance the same values. The theme was "A Time of Opportunity."

The point was that it was a "time of opportunity" not only for the donor and for the college, but for the nation as well. President Reagan had just taken office, and the business community was extraordinarily optimistic about the future.

The trustee was quoted in the case for his wisdom and encouragement. Partly because he had played an important role in building the case, and saw his own deepest aspirations reflected in the college's development program, he became an even more enthusiastic advocate. He was instrumental in bringing the campaign, the largest ever attempted by the school, to a highly successful conclusion.

Because this man was moved both intellectually and emotionally, he had developed a sense of ownership of the college and its program. He acted with conviction because he felt that he was promoting his own best interests—and those of the college, the nation and civilization itself.

That's how much an effective case can accomplish. A list of needs or tired slogans about "continuing the traditions?" Instead, the case that seeks out the person's responsive chord, and resonates with it, is the case that compels action.

II

Getting
People Involved

The way to raise

real money is to provide

real involvement. So put

people before dollars.

8

Go for the Gold

THE BEST PERSON TO LEAD your program is the one who has a reputation for allowing nothing to fail.

This type of leader— the type whose presence creates confidence—is rare.

Most volunteers can be grouped into three other categories: the *responsible* (those we can rely on to follow through); the *responsive* (those we can hope to move); and the *unresponsive*. "Si" Seymour says of this last group: "The finest rhetoric never reaches these people, if only because they are not there to listen."

People have been trying for centuries, without success, to change a lump of lead into a nugget of gold. In enlisting volunteer leadership, it's best to begin by "going for the gold"—the winners. After that, perhaps, some alchemy can be used to develop the *next* generation of leaders.

"One of the best ways to predict the success or failure of any fund-raising program," says one veteran development officer, "is to ask: Have people of stature been enlisted as active members of the team?'"

Respected people doing a first-rate job—that breeds achievement.

Influence flows downward, so begin at the top. It's easier to enlist the vice president, for example, if you've already enlisted the president—not the other way around.

What makes for good leadership? Most experienced fund-raisers look for these qualities:

1. Affluence—the ability to make a substantial contribution.
2. Influence—the ability to attract others to volunteer and to make substantial contributions.
3. Availability—the willingness to give priority attention to the program.
4. Team spirit—the willingness to provide voluntary leadership and to accept professional direction.

Some would add to this list "interest in the cause." While this is certainly helpful, it's secondary. If interest is already present, wonderful. If not, it can be developed.

Those who are already close to your cause are the obvious choices, and may be easier to enlist. If they meet the four criteria, you want them on your team. People will certainly expect the board members, for example, to be active.

But by enlisting people who are identified with the community—not necessarily with the cause—you'll help to build a sense that it's the community's enterprise, not just a self-serving effort by the organization.

For example, when the board of a small Catholic hospital tapped a non-Catholic to lead its campaign, the response from the community was unusually enthusiastic.

"He's not on the board," people said. "He's not even Catholic." This enlistment succeeded in communicating to people that the project was important to the town, beyond the organization's provincial concerns.

When the campaign headquarters is placed in a bank building, rather than "on campus," or when the campaign chairman uses personal letterhead, rather than the organization's, the same message comes through.

The most successful organizations are those that make their program the *community's*—and who pass the torch of leadership and ownership to those who can make things happen for the organization and community.

"Going for the gold," and getting it, isn't easy. The most respected leaders are in short supply, busy and sought after. In a way, you're competing more for volunteers than for money.

"It's easy to get people to give," says Samuel Belzburg, Chairman of First City Financial in Vancouver. "What's tough is to get them to ask." When you put the giver and asker together in one person, then you have success.

In our quest to enlist such leaders, we want to be as thoughtful, strategic and persistent as we are in inviting a seven-figure contribution. (In fact, if we've thought it through, our candidates for the top leadership posts may well be those who can use their financial capabilities to make pacesetting pledges, which in turn will make their leading all the more effective and easy.)

In the enlistment of volunteer leadership, it's best not to take the path of least resistance. Go for the gold; you just might get it.

9

Create Authentic Involvement

INVOLVEMENT, IT IS SAID, is more important than information. If we want people to invest their time and resources in a program, we'll want to give them *authentic* involvement in the cause.

"Pretend participation"—a name on a letterhead—isn't enough. Neither is a seat on a board that has no important function. True leaders easily see through these ploys.

We want people to feel involved with our causes the same way they are involved with their families, their work, their religion. The volunteer deserves to feel that the organization is a vital part of their everyday life.

The best way to develop that sense of involvement is to invite a person to *do something important* for us—something they are especially qualified and suited to do.

The person will then begin to become an *insider*. Once that happens, they will have a greater stake in the success of the organization—and a greater willingness to contribute to that success.

Take, for example, a trustee of a certain university in a medium-sized industrial city. He had been on the board for a few years. A respected gentleman and president of a Fortune 500 company, he had no reason to do much more for the university than attend the semiannual board meetings.

When a capital campaign was contemplated, it was clear that he would be interviewed in the study. His views would be important because of who he was in his own right. He also represented the type of people who would be vital to become part of this enterprise, if it were to achieve its goal.

The university benefited from the interview—not only because of what it learned, but because the act of consulting this executive for his views increased his involvement.

Following the study, he was invited to serve on the development committee of the board. Through this role, he became even more of an insider. The members of this group were to review and approve the university's ten-year development plan, and each agreed to host a meeting of a small group of community leaders to discuss the plan.

Not long after joining this committee, the executive agreed to serve as general chairman of the campaign. He had become genuinely involved in the school.

This involvement increased as he provided the benefit of his thinking to setting the campaign goal, identifying prospective donors and evaluating their capacity to give. He also identified prospective volunteers, enlisted them and asked them to contribute.

As the general chairman, he often worked in a team with the university president and other key volunteers. The more people who joined in enlisting and inviting investment, the more widely the case was made, and the more people had a stake in the success of the program.

A donor's involvement can go beyond raising money. In fact, when people take part in the general business of an organization, they become more committed to its success. One could argue that a major donor deserves to have as much to say about the future of the organization as a major stockholder does about the future of the company. As investors, both are entitled to influence the setting of policy.

This principle of authentic involvement applies before, during and after raising funds. It is the best way to invite someone (who deserves the role) from being an outsider to being an insider—and finally to enable that person to engage and develop *ownership* in the organization.

This is a basic *quid pro quo* in the enterprise of development. Too many organizations still try to get around it. If we want real dollars and real work from people, then it's up to us to provide them with real involvement. If we want token dollars and token work, then we can provide token involvement.

10

The Process of Planning is More Important Than the Plan Itself

WITHOUT A STRATEGY based on a knowledge of the philanthropic community, there will be only random ideas without a guiding purpose. As the Roman philosopher Seneca said, "When a man does not know what harbor he is making for, no wind is the right wind."

Or, as Yogi Berra put it more recently, "You've got to be very careful if you don't know where you are going, because you might not get there."

So an organization creates a plan for its future—particularly when it's preparing to embark on a fund-raising campaign or a long-range development program. The act of planning also focuses and clarifies the thinking. This is another way in which the process itself is more important than the resulting document.

The beginning of a development program, especially a capital campaign, automatically attracts attention. Getting ready for the program provides a special opportunity to rethink priorities, recommit loyalties and redirect energies.

What makes planning even more valuable is the opportunity it presents for good old *involvement.* "The primary benefit of the planning process is the process itself, and not a plan," writes George A. Steiner in *Strategic Planning.* If an organization's leaders are on the ball, they will use the planning process to get people involved in mapping the organization's future—especially those people who have the power to help *bring about* that future.

Authentic involvement in the planning process can promote a sense of ownership among prospective donors and volunteers. People are simply more motivated to work for, and invest in, the realization of plans they themselves have helped to develop.

(There is, of course, a time when the focus shifts from planning to implementation. Beware of "paralysis by analysis.")

Most donors want to be assured that your "have your ducks in a row," and are satisfied to know that you can get all of the details for them if they ask. They want to be shown that you're using the skills of the world of management, and that you're treating your enterprise in an intentional, organized and strategic manner.

This kind of planning is exactly what one philanthropist wanted when he asked a hospital trustee:

"What's your mission? And I don't mean that formal stuff, either. What *are* you doing? What does your five-year plan look like? What services are you going to add? To abandon?

More and more donors are asking these tough questions.

—⁓—

Let's be clear: What we're talking about isn't the kind of "long-range planning" that has been popular to so long, but real strategic planning. The difference is important.

Traditional planning is an administrative tool. Predictions are made on the basis of past performance, current resources and demographic trends.

Strategic planning is an entrepreneurial process. The organization attempts to design its own future—based on its strengths and the external environment, its opportunities and constraints. Strategic planning looks at forces outside the organization's control, forces like rising expectations for health care or a declining industrial base.

Through this kind of planning, the organization examines its options; decides what its future directions can be; and develops an action plan, a budget and a timetable for meeting its objectives.

Any organization engaged in a structured development program also writes a *fund-raising plan*. Again, the thinking of key volunteers may be reflected in this plan, which is designed by a competent professional.

With these kinds of plans, an organization is seen as a quality operation—an intelligently managed enterprise, aware of its purpose and its environment, and ready to take advantage of opportunities as they arise. This kind of organization, in short, looks like a smart investment.

Without these plans, an organization remains one of thousands that struggle on from one year to the next, hoping to be able to continue to do what they've done before. In today's environment, this kind of organization is a high risk investment.

So, take a look around. Get the right kinds of people involved in your planning process. More than likely, they'll put their money on the plans they helped to build.

11

Share Your Plans Without Asking for Money

A "LIST OF NEEDS" where it's obvious that a writer was asked to organize them into a program and give them a unifying purpose, that's not in your best interest.

A campaign with untested goals and unidentified leaders is a campaign that is not in your best interest.

Using your planning process, you've decided what your financial objectives will be. Now, to find out *if* the funds can be raised—and *how* they can be raised—it's time that you share your plans with the donor community.

How do you go about getting an accurate reading without submitting to "trial by fire"—that is, without actually asking for the money?

The standard procedure is to conduct a feasibility study, discussed in the following pages. Another is the cultivation or "awareness" program.

Sitting across from a development executive at a meeting one day was an estate planner. At a similar meeting at lunch the next day, an attorney and an accountant were in attendance. These people were on hand to take part in a series of small-group meetings being sponsored by the community's largest hospital.

The purpose was to address several major health care issues, and to discuss the hospital's plans for responding to these issues. The hospital was intent on getting the benefit of the guests' thinking.

These meetings were designed primarily for major donors. While our three professionals could make significant gifts in their own right, the real reason for inviting them was that they were counselors to the best prospective donors in the community.

Little did anyone know, however, that they would come to play such an important role in the hospital's development program. For they turned out to be the three major advisors for one of the hospital's top prospective donors.

This person also attended one of the meetings. Later, with his three advisors, he worked out a plan that resulted in a $1 million commitment to the hospital.

What made this series of meetings especially effective was their dual purpose: not only to provide information, but also to obtain the views of the guests. In this way, the development program could be built in concert with their concerns and interests.

—◦◦◦—

From the organization's perspective, such a series of meetings might be called a "cultivation" program. From the donor's point of view, something along the lines of a "leadership awareness program" is more appealing.

The idea is to share the organization's plans in an unpretentious, small-group setting, with plenty of time for reactions, questions and discussion. No funds are solicited, and no one is asked to volunteer—but a lot can be accomplished.

This process can give an organization what one executive calls a "reality fix." That is, you'll find out what the leaders in your community think of your organization and its plans, and what concerns you'll want to deal with.

The traditional cultivation program is most often used to help an organization find out whether it can attain a certain financial objective. But such a program can tell you much more. In fact, you can determine how to reach your goal, based on a knowledge of the donor community and specific donors—as well as the dynamics that might be brought into play between Donor A and Donor B.

These are the kinds of insights that can help you put together an effective fund-raising strategy.

And there's another benefit: For people to be able to provide informed responses, they will usually recognize that they want to know about your organization and its plans (however tentative).

Because of their desire to know, they're likely to be receptive listeners. This gives you an excellent opportunity to briefly present your case—test market it, if you will—at a time when funds are not being solicited, and when their thinking can influence yours.

This approach seeks to cultivate relationships with donors by *involving* them—the best kind of cultivation. There are other ways that can also be effective.

One method is direct mail. This vehicle can be used to provide information through a series of letters or publications; or to solicit memberships or small contributions. The purpose is to stimulate interest and to attract new donors, some of whom may become major donors down the line.

Another method of cultivation includes all the activities that come under the heading of public relations. These include news coverage in the print and broadcast media, editorials, public service advertising, a speakers' bureau for community groups and organizations, and benefits and special events.

The primary advantage of these activities is that they keep your organization's good work in the public eye—most importantly the eye of your donors. They are *not* a substitute for face-to-face cultivation activities that promote dialogue. But they can support it. They can create a favorable climate for raising money.

12

Use a Feasibility Study
to Build a Strategy

ONCE PEOPLE HAVE HELPED us to shape our development plans, we want to ask them what they are willing to *do* to help transform the plans into realities.

The courteous and elegant way to find out this kind of information—without "putting the arm" on anyone—is to conduct a series of *confidential*, one-on-one interviews.

Some practitioners are wedded to the more limited and traditional purpose of the study: to test the feasibility of reaching the dollar goal, period.

But a study can do much more than this. It's a very effective way to *listen to and involve* people who will be crucial to the success of the program.

With the information and insights gained through the study, we can begin to build an overall strategy for the effort. Equally important, we can start to think in term of specific *tactics*—that is, how to best approach a certain person in a way they'd like to be approached.

For the study can go even further than the leadership awareness program in providing a golden opportunity to learn each person's attitude toward the organization and its plans. Within the total program, which projects does the prospective donor favor, and why? Is the person likely to contribute to one of these projects? Are they likely to become a volunteer and seek contributions? A campaign leader?

A study enables us to get the answers "from the horse's mouth," so to speak. A study can tell us whether the organization is ready to embark on a program. We can find out what people consider to be the strengths and weaknesses of the case and program. We can identify donors for pace-setting contributions, and often learn what they think.

The study, in fact, can be seen as "the first call for money"—the first step in the marketing of the upcoming campaign. In a quiet, dignified way, the study puts people on alert. It can even start the wheels turning.

A few years ago, an Illinois hospital conducted a study to determine the feasibility of a $2.8 million campaign. Among those interviewed in the small town was the president of its largest company.

During the interview, the company president was shown a "standards chart" that indicated the size and number of commitments—based on past experience— that would be required to raise $2.8 million.

The top investment would have to be $500,000.

"Although I'm not seeking a commitment," said the interviewer, "I do want your opinion on whether these standards can be achieved. Do you see your company as being among the top five gifts on the chart?"

"Yes," the executive answered, "but the validity of these standards is critical." He kept prodding: "Are you sure these figures are reliable? Can we raise $2.8 million without reaching these standards?"

At the time, the interviewer wasn't sure exactly why this gentleman was so concerned with the levels of investment that would be required. He did reassure the company president that the standards *were* an accurate predictor of success.

—⌇⌇⌇—

While the interviewer was finishing his study and writing his report, the company president went to work behind the scenes to line up the necessary support within his firm for a $500,000 pledge. All this took place before it had even been determined that the hospital could conduct a successful campaign.

Three months before the campaign was announced, the company confirmed that the hospital could count on a $500,000 commitment. The hospital went on to raise its $2.8 million—ahead of schedule.

What was remarkable about this experience is that the very *process* of conducting the feasibility study may have done more for the success of the campaign than did all the information that was obtained, and all the strategy that was built upon it.

It's not unusual for this kind of thing to happen when an organization involves the right people in its plans for development. What's important is for us to *hear* those people who can make our program work. After all, it is *their* community. It is *their* hospital. The way we go about it—through a strategic planning process, a cultivation program or a formal feasibility study—is secondary. (In fact, we may use all three of these methods in a sequence.)

In the final analysis, if you've given your prospective donors some kind of opportunity to tell you what they want—and especially if you've responded to their interests—you'll be in a strong position to develop a sense of commitment to your program.

We couldn't say it any better than Aldous Huxley did: "It's not very difficult to persuade people to do what they already long to do."

III

Setting the Pace for Giving

If the most capable give

substantially and give early,

the others will follow,

as night follows day.

13

If You Seek Average Gifts,
You Get Below-Average Results

YOU CAN'T JUMP ACROSS a chasm in two equal leaps and expect to have any followers.

People who are new to development often think in terms of "average" gifts. They have somehow gotten it into their heads that what you do is divide the goal by the number of likely donors, then ask everyone to give the same amount.

For example, if the goal is $1 million, and there are 200 good prospective donors, someone will suggest that each person be asked for $5,000. The idea is to reach the goal through 100 per cent participation at the $5,000 level.

Assuming that everyone can easily afford to give $5,000, this sounds like it would make the volunteer's job easier. But seeking average gifts produces below average results. In fact, it is certain to lead to failure.

One problem with raising money by the multiplication table—$5,000 times 200—is that not everyone will participate. We'd like to think they will, but they won't. Even worse, seeking $5,000 from each donor will, in effect, set a ceiling on what an inspired donor may want to pledge.

Tolstoy described this phenomenon in *War and Peace* (yes, I really read its 1456 pages for philanthropic lessons!): "The distinguished dignitary who bore the title of 'Collector of Alms' went round to all the brothers. Pierre would have liked to subscribe all he had, but, fearing that it might look like pride, subscribed the same amount as the others."

Let's say someone you know pledges $5,000. You feel that because of the person's financial circumstances, they are twice as capable as you. Are you likely to pledge $5,000? We all tend to give in relation to what others are giving.

"One hundred per cent participation" has a nice ring to it, but doesn't work much better than seeking average gifts. When the word gets out that the objective is to get *everyone* to give, no matter how much, some people will give as little as they can. This tokenism will lower the sights of the leaders, and you'll raise less money.

Finally, the "averaging" approach assumes that twenty pledges of $5,000 each, taken together, will have the same impact as a single pledge of $100,000. Not so. In the raising of money, the commitment that really counts is not the average one or the token one. It's the *leadership* commitment that sets great things in motion.

14

A Few Will Do the Most

"What's the status of our top ten?"

Anyone who has worked with a first-rate development professional knows well the sound of these words. For the most successful people in this work are known for focusing on the few who will do the most—the small number of people who will produce the greatest results.

The professionals know from experience that in most programs, ninety per cent of the funds come from about ten per cent of the donors.

This interesting phenomenon seems to be almost universal. People in sales often say that ninety per cent of their dollar volume comes from ten per cent of their customers.

Just as the salesman spends most of his time on his big customers, we devote most of our efforts to the major donors. We ask again and again, "What's the status of our top ten?" For what these folks do is going to make or break the program.

From studying the giving patterns of past campaigns, we've learned a lot more about how many will it take, giving how much, in order to attain the goal. To help direct the energies of volunteers, this wisdom is typically set forth on a single sheet full of numbers—numbers of a significance that can hardly be overstated.

This document, the "standards chart" or "table of investments," lists the number of contributions at various levels that have been found to take to reach the goal.

For example, most successful $1 million campaigns have had a top commitment of $100,000, or ten per cent. Typically, you also want to secure two contributions at the $75,000 level; three at the $50,000 level; and four at the $25,000 level. These ten commitments total $400,000, or 40 per cent of the goal.

The next 100 commitments would account for another thirty or forty per cent of the goal; "numerous others" will generate the balance.

This is called the "rule of the thirds." To wit: One-third of the goal is usually raised from each group—the top ten, the next 100 and everybody else.

The rule, of course, is applied with some flexibility. The numbers on the standards chart are adjusted somewhat, according to the type of organization and the giving history of the community. In some cases, it will take the top donor getting you 20 per cent of the way home, and it may take the top ten contributing fifty to sixty per cent of the total.

The standards chart also helps you figure out how many people will be visited. Normally, to secure each commitment, you'll want two to four prospective donors.

If you know how many prospective donors you want, it's easy to get from there to the number of volunteers you would enlist. Divide the total number of people by five. This assumes that the volunteers themselves will be contributors, and that each will call on four others, which is probably the most you'll want to assign to anyone.

———◈———

Where will you find your best prospective donors? Experience shows that the best donors for the immediate future are those who have given in the past. "Remember that the best prospects are those who have already given," said Si Seymour, "and that the more a person gives, the more likely he is to give more."

New donors, of course, are always necessary in order to replenish the pool of contributors and one may even surprise everyone by setting a new and higher standard. Always concentrate your efforts on the few who will do the most. Then you'll have the luxury of broadening your base—the "grassroots" donors who will someday become your new top ten.

15

The Early Donor Sets the Pace

"He who gives early gives twice."

—*Cervantes*

I ONCE OFFERED CERVANTES' WORDS to a new chair of a board. With a twinkle in his eye, he said, "That's great. Then we can hit him up again."

Well, I had something else in mind.

The point is not that he who gives early should quickly be asked to give again—but that their contribution can set an example for others to follow.

If those who give early also give at the higher levels, so much the better. Major commitments that are made later are wonderful, but they don't have the same pace-setting power as ones made early in the process. We want contributions to have a chance to communicate.

This dynamic is what makes the beginning of a program a time of special opportunity.

Let's pick a number and say that the first contribution to a campaign comes in at $2,000, instead of the $1,000 that was expected. The next person to make a commitment may well give $1,500 instead of the $750 they were considering. This can create a ripple effect that carries through the ranks.

Of course, a "negative ripple effect" can also occur. If the first contribution comes in at $500, instead of the anticipated $1,000, then the next person might decide to give only $250, rather than $500.

In either case, it's the people who give first who set the pattern for those who follow. So it pays to devote a lot of thought to the order in which they are approached.

———

Ben Franklin's 200-year-old formula for success has held up so well that one director of development we know makes a point of quoting it to every group of volunteers he works with:

"My practice," explained Franklin, "is to go first to those who may be counted upon to be favorable, who know the cause and believe in it, and ask them to give as generously as possible. When they have done so, I go next to those who may be presumed to have a favorable opinion and to be disposed to listening, and secure their adherence."

"Lastly, I go to those who know little of the matter or have no known predilection for it and influence them by presentation of the names of those who have already given."

Our institutions, agencies and organizations still follow this advice. But now we structure our programs so that the very first people we see are those who are not only the closest to the cause but also (as I've been saying) the most likely to contribute at the highest levels, relative to their capacity.

The first people to be visited are often grouped into a "pacesetters" or "advance giving" division. This group can actually include people at various financial levels who have been selected because we expect that they will serve as examples for their peers.

How moving and inspiring it can be when a custodian on the college staff pledges $5,000 to "his" school. Certainly, this kind of sacrifice can motivate others in circumstances like his. But it can also set an example for others with a greater capacity who hear about the custodian's commitment. They'll see it as the best evidence that this school is loved and worth investing in.

So first, identify people who are likely to make commitments that are large for their financial circumstances. Call on these folks before anyone else, so the news of their commitments will encourage the rest to join in. Those who stepped to the forefront will then have the reward of watching others follow their lead.

16

Trustees Have an Opportunity, Not an Obligation

OTHER DONORS WILL ALWAYS look to the trustees to set the process in motion. People will always ask, and with good reason: "What did the board do?"

Whatever example the board sets, the effect will be felt throughout the enterprise. "As the board goes," according to the old saying, "so goes the campaign."

This does not mean, however, that the trustees are pressured. How dismaying it is to hear "It's the rent you pay for the space you take," or "It's give, get or get off."

Trusteeship presents an *opportunity*, not an obligation. The trustee's commitment is voluntary. It is an expression of leadership.

The board member carries the torch of voluntarism and lights the path for others. James F. Oates, former chairman of the Equitable Life Assurance Society of the United States, made it clear: "The trustees have to lead in acts and deeds, as well as in words and titles."

After serving as general chairman of a successful campaign for Princeton University, Mr. Oates said, "I think if I had to select the one most important decision we made during this campaign, it was the decision that we would not publicly announce it or start it until every trustee—*every trustee*—had made a substantial, sacrificial gift. You can't expect to have a following without that leadership."

The same kind of opportunity presents itself to those leaders who serve on a development committee, such as the "campaign cabinet," and who may or may not be board members. This group includes those who will be asking others to give. They have an excellent opportunity to lead the way by their deeds.

But from the ranks of the trustees and the campaign cabinet, a dangerous idea may be expressed. Someone is likely to ask, "If a person can *raise* a lot of money, isn't that person valuable—even if their personal gift isn't much?" Or "She won't give, but she can deliver her corporate gift."

Not really. First, the person who asks another to make a greater sacrifice than they have made is not setting the best kind of precedent. Second, and even more importantly, this person is investing time and energy in the program—but without exercising the *maximum influence* at their disposal. The volunteer who invites others to invest without the benefit of a strong personal example is like the shoemaker who goes without shoes.

It's certainly easy enough to understand, however, why many trustees are reluctant donors—and why many boards fail to set a strong example as a group.

Some organizations enlist trustees without regard for their affluence and influence. There's nothing wrong with enlisting a board member because of the constituency that person represents, or because of the special expertise they can bring to the board. But fund-raising miracles rarely come from this kind of trustee.

Other organizations do enlist people who have the capacity to contribute and to raise money. But then the organization fails to involve them or give them anything meaningful to do—until it's campaign time.

We want trustees to have an important role in the organization. We want them to have a chance to develop their rightful sense of ownership. Members of a "rubber-stamp" board may well think of raising money as an administrative function. Little wonder if they aren't responsive to lofty rhetoric about "leadership" when there's money to be raised.

17

Staff Giving Can Lend Credibility

"Why bother to solicit the staff? There's not much money in it, is there?"

(When the original edition book was released, staff giving was typically recommended by counsel in campaigns. Today, the idea is more controversial, yet it's a notion that still has merit for many organizations.)

If the staff has an opportunity to give, and responds at a high level in relation to their capacity, you've gained much more than dollars.

First, staff contributions can have a powerful impact on the rest of your donor constituency.

Together with the board and other volunteer groups, the staff is part of the "official family" of the organization. Their commitment provides others with a clear indication that those who are most intimate with the organization—those who see it every day—*do* believe in its value and respect its leadership. Through their actions, they attest to the wisdom of the development effort.

There's another benefit that may be even more important to the future of the organization. A museum curator once told me, "I think our involvement is very good for staff spirit. We feel like we're a part of the development effort—that we're helping to make this museum an even better place to work."

A development effort can get an extra boost when it is a *total effort* of the total organization. A campaign presents an opportunity for everyone in the official family to become involved in building the organization's future—to become an "ambassador for development." Everyone who will benefit from the success of the program deserves a chance to invest in it and to work for it.

Too often, however, the staff isn't approached in this spirit. Instead, they're made to feel that their giving is a requirement, rather than an opportunity. As employees, they may feel that their jobs, salaries or promotions may be at stake.

That kind of approach will backfire every time. In asking anyone for money, but especially when a peer among the staff invites investment, we take seriously the premise that giving is *voluntary*. And in the case of staff, their investing of their working lives in the future of the organization, often at financial sacrifice, may be the greatest contribution, worthy of acknowledgement.

18

Make Great Investments Possible

NOT LONG AGO, a prominent family in a small Northern industrial city made a $2 million commitment to the city's leading university.

The impact of this kind of investment can hardly be measured. In this case, it was the largest philanthropic investment ever made in that part of the state. Many people asked, "How did they manage so much?"

The fact is that if the pledge made to a capital campaign had to be paid in cash, the family might never have done it. The investment was made possible by a combination of several devices, including a subscription period and the use of financial vehicle other than cash.

How can these kinds of ideas be used in your program?

■ Provide donors flexible payment terms through a *subscription period*. This will allow them to spread the payments, and the tax benefits, over a period of years. In this way, the donor can often make a larger commitment.

- A person or a company that can write a check for $50,000 can usually pledge $150,000 over a three-year period. Board members are often offered a five-year pledge period, and we're beginning to see commitments made that will be fulfilled over a period of as much as ten years.

- Provide donors with flexibility and choices in the *financial vehicle* they can use to make their commitments. Certain instruments (appreciated securities, trusts, real estate or insurance policies) can have distinct tax advantages. These more creative vehicles can also enable donors to hold the assets or retain the income to provide for their own security.

Tax savings are rarely the major motivation for donors. Once the decision to contribute has been made, however, the savings can allow the donor to make a greater commitment at less actual cost.

- Provide donors with recognition through a program of *named commemorative opportunities*. Such a program offers tangible and public recognition for major investments, through the naming of physical facilities, scholarships and the like.

Commemorative opportunities are used to suggest a particular level of investment, and often to "raise the sights" of the donor. For example, instead of asking the person for a commitment of $140,000, it is suggested that for $150,000, a program or project, perhaps a physical space, can be named in honor of the donor, a family, another individual, or a corporation.

Such a proposal is best received when it is tailored to the interests of the donor.

A variation on this theme is the use of giving clubs in annual programs. (No, that's not what you hit someone with to get them to give.) Several clubs are created for those who contribute at different levels. Those who increase their commitments move up into the more prestigious clubs. Those at the top levels may receive such benefits as an annual dinner with the chief executive officer, or special access to the organization's facilities and services.

■ Provide donors with opportunities for *planned giving*. Together with capital campaigns and annual programs, planned (or "deferred") giving has become one of the three basic supports for the philanthropic tripod.

By arranging for a deferred payment, often to be made after death, the donor is often able to make a greater commitment than they ever would have expected.

The old adage, "He who advocates must first bequeath," is becoming more of a reality. This effort, like most others, is best led by example; when trustees do it, others will follow.

Cultivate relationships with trust officers, accountants and attorneys so that they will be receptive to the idea of planned giving when a client brings it up—or they may take the initiative—and be willing to provide the necessary technical assistance. But rely on the development staff to inform the appropriate prospective donors about the benefits of planned giving, and to attract them to the program.

Use these various tools, separately or in combination, to make it easier for donors to do the great things they want to do. If there's a will, so to speak, there's probably a way.

IV

Applying the Campaign Principle

*Structure makes people
more productive. It gives them
standards against which
they can measure their
performance.*

19

People Prefer Structure

ASKING PEOPLE TO WORK in an "unstructured" setting is like sending them out to find polar bears in a
snowstorm.

If you want people to be effective, you'll want to
give them a structure. You'll want them to have a way to
measure performance and results—something against
which to shine.

Human beings work best with goals and deadlines.
They want to know what is expected of them, and where
they fit into the big picture.

The person responsible for directing the program
provides the volunteers with this kind of structure.

This is especially vital because campaign management is *project* management. It calls for building an
organization to accomplish a specific purpose over a
limited period of time.

Some organizations just pull together a bunch of
people and turn them loose with names. It comes as
no surprise that ambiguous plans produce ambiguous
results.

An example of specificity is when volunteers are
asked to assume definite and limited jobs. The way to

enlist a busy community leader is to hand the person a job description—a list of four or five tasks that are important, along with a timetable.

The way not to enlist that leader is to say, "Well, we need X thousand dollars, and we'd like you to help out. There won't be a lot of meetings, though—just a couple of cards." People with experience raising money know where that leads. The others will soon find out.

Most of the nitty-gritty work of a development program is accomplished through committees. But people aren't enlisted by asking them to join a committee. One of the best enlistments I ever heard went like this': "Because you're a leader in this community, I feel that you, as I do, have a sense of obligation—really a sense of opportunity—to do this important job." And it was followed by what the group was going to achieve that would, in the end, matter to the community.

For people to work effectively within our structure, we also want to create a *positive climate*—a climate of optimism, enthusiasm and confidence. Without this kind of atmosphere, assignments and deadlines count for little.

Good things rarely happen in a bad atmosphere. Once in a while, someone will express the notion that people will perform better if we tell them how badly things are going. That's the wrong approach to management, especially the management of volunteers.

We want to give people the same sense that Pogo, the comic strip character, did when he proclaimed: "We're faced with insurmountable opportunity."

In short, we don't try to shame or coerce people into performing. We build a structure to direct people; to channel their energies; to bring out the *best* in them.

20

Take One Step at a Time

"NOTHING IS PARTICULARLY HARD," said Henry Ford, "if you divide it into small jobs."

The task of building 100,000 cars—or raising a million dollars—can appear staggering, until it is broken down into a series of small and logical steps.

This is an excellent reason for placing *one professional* in charge of managing a development program— someone who has the overview, knows the steps and can direct the volunteers.

"A successful development effort results from a series of steps, taken one at a time, each done in correct sequence, according to a plan and schedule," explains James A. Jones, a consultant who has conducted in-depth studies of hundreds of campaigns.

"At any one time," says Mr. Jones, "people should be concerned with only one step. When a step is improperly taken, the next will be more difficult. When a step is correctly made, the next will be easier and more effective."

By taking one step at a time, you make the larger, more complex tasks manageable. You give your volunteers a fresh sense of accomplishment every day.

This rule applies on every level—from the assignments given to each volunteer to the major milestones in the overall progress of a campaign.

For example, each division (or group of prospective donors) is visited in sequence, to set the best possible pace for the effort. Prospective donors for six-figure contributions are seen *before* five-figure donors. In this way, the highest-level folks will set the pattern for those who follow.

Even in inviting the investment of a single person, there are specific steps to be taken in sequence. Before the person is invited to invest, they deserve to be informed about the *program*. And before the volunteer makes the call, they deserve to be informed about the *prospective donor*.

The proper pacing of a development program is both a science and an art. Volunteers often feel that the development officer or campaign director is moving too slowly. The professional often feels that the volunteers want to jump the gun. Depending on the situation, either may be right.

21

Scheduling Creates Momentum

A FUND-RAISING PROGRAM is run with the knowledge that people's attention spans are limited.

This is no reflection on our volunteers; it's just a fact of life. Development professionals are a bit of a master of ceremonies. They develop a schedule that keeps people fired up and excited, never allowing boredom to set in, and making sure the whole show is brought to a close before the audience gets tired.

How do you keep the excitement high? One principle to keep in mind is *synergy*.

Buckminster Fuller borrowed this term from metallurgy. If three metals, for example, are combined to form an alloy, the strength of the alloy can be greater than the sum of the strengths of the three component metals. Fuller extended this concept to any situation where, one might say, "the whole is greater than the sum of its parts."

A campaign is one such situation. When three events—for example, three major commitments—happen at the same time, or in rapid succession, they can have a powerful impact on the campaign, far more than if the three events had occurred a couple of weeks apart. The point is that synergy gets people excited.

Something like this may happen by serendipity. But as the veteran fund-raiser knows, nine times out of ten, it's all been carefully orchestrated in advance.

Scheduling events to create momentum calls for a lot of behind-the-scenes work. That means investing more resources in the development program, especially upfront, when the outgo of funds far exceeds the income. The more you invest, the more the reward. That goes for time as well as money.

Once the curtain goes up and the program is announced, there is a rush of activity. For the campaign director, of course, the pace is often maddening to sustain. As Lewis Carroll observed:

"You see, it takes all the running you can do to keep in the same place. If you want to get somewhere else, you must run at least twice as fast as that!"

22

Build a Sense of Campaign

THE WINNERS OF THIS WORLD are those who set a goal, set a deadline, and place milestones along the way.

In campaigning, they ask people to serve in a leadership structure. They ask them to contribute to specific programs.

These are some of the hallmarks of a campaign, the greatest invention in fund-raising since the bake sale. These are the structures and dynamics that will, in fact, enhance any development enterprise—and, for that matter, just about any human endeavor.

The dynamics that come into play during intense campaign activity can be truly exhilarating. Some people will even love the campaign more than the cause. It's anything but "business as usual."

To sustain the excitement, to keep the adrenalin flowing, is as necessary as it is nerve-wracking. Will we win? Oscar Wilde understood the ironic task of the campaign director: "The suspense is terrible. I hope it will last."

So cultivate the passions. Make them eager for the contest.

23

Create a Climate of Universality

"Public sentiment is everything.
With public sentiment, nothing can fail.
Without it, nothing can succeed."

—*Abraham Lincoln*

DEVELOPMENT PROGRAMS prosper in a climate of universality. One reason the concept of a campaign works so well is that everyone in the community can join in: individuals, corporations, foundations, clubs, unions, churches and even (praise be !) governments.

The more good people you can get into the parade, the better. Spread the work among the largest possible group of *effective* volunteers.

This will produce two results: An individual is more likely to "join up," knowing that their load will be manageable. And because more people get involved with the destiny of the organization, a sense of "rightness" and inevitable success will develop. Besides, the more "insiders" who claim a sense of ownership, the better.

You may raise 90 per cent of your goal from a handful of donors. But don't stop there. Give more people a chance to get in on the action. Even if you spend more than you raise in order to do this, the intangible benefits make it well worth the effort. Besides, the next time around, the little giver may become a big investor.

It's not a very good idea, though, to do as the chairman of a prominent school once did. He admonished his director of development to enlist three times as many volunteers as necessary—because he felt that when one or two didn't produce, the job might still get done.

The better way is to try to enlist those who you think will take seriously their assignments. Otherwise, a few who are less serious can drag everyone else down, and defeat the momentum and enthusiasm that's building.

Be selective. Enlist people who are known for coming through. Plan for the best in people, not the worst. What you plan for is what you're likely to get.

24

Winning Is Fundamental

YOU CAN'T GET RESULTS if you don't know where you're going. Set a dollar goal for your program—and set smaller goals along the way. Beware of the turtle who said, "I'm glad I'm going so slowly, because I'm not sure I'm headed in the right direction."

We all achieve more when we have objectives. "Before you can score," says a Greek proverb, "you must first have a goal."

You want the goal to be high enough to stretch people, and low enough for them to reach. "When setting an objective for a campaign," says R. Blair Schreyer, president of Ketchum, Inc., "it is better to have a believable objective in which everyone has confidence. The probability is that you can oversubscribe a believable goal, but you will, almost without exception, undersubscribe an unbelievable goal."

Winning may not be everything. A program that falls short of its goal may indeed raise a lot of money, win new friends for an organization, and enable it to do more than before. But being seen as successful in something that people are familiar with and see as measurable (raising money) brings untold reward.

25

Meetings Keep Things Moving

"NOT *ANOTHER* MEETING!"

It's true. In every campaign, as in every other human enterprise, there are too many meetings. But that's because they *work*.

Meetings are the glue that keeps a development program together. Experience has shown that a person's effectiveness as a volunteer is directly related to their attendance at meetings. (That's why we can dip beneath the high-purpose essentials in this book to include one that *seems* small and *seems* mundane.)

Meetings accomplish a number of things:

- They provide opportunities to inform, stimulate, inspire and recognize people.
- They instill a positive, shared sense of responsibility among the people in attendance.
- They provide deadlines. To have something to talk about, you have to have *done* something. (We human beings are less likely to accomplish that which we have plenty of time to accomplish.)

But how do you get people to come—so they can receive these fine benefits?

- Make sure the leaders treat the meeting as important.
- Start and stop on time.
- Always provide substance.
- If substance or attendance is lacking, postpone the meeting.

Meetings, of course, aren't the only way to get things done. If you use the other ways, too—the memo, the phone call, the personal visit—people are more likely to feel that any given meeting will be worth attending.

In the end, meetings have a lot to do with how people view the organization. Well-run and well-attended meetings provide tangible evidence of an effective organization and a strong development program.

V

Asking
for Money

The volunteer is an

investment counselor—

not a salesman.

26

People Give to People

PEOPLE DON'T GIVE to an institution, an agency or an organization. They give to the person who asks them. Often, a contribution is made because of how one person feels about another. The organization may be almost incidental.

People also give *for* people—not for endowments or swimming pools.

Real money cannot be raised without people. At the outset of any campaign, someone will always say, "The money's out there." But the mere existence of money, without people to move it into action, is of little consequence.

The donor, too, is always a person. A foundation, corporation or committee never makes a decision. Only people make decisions.

It is true, of course, that foundation proposals are expected to follow the foundation's guidelines. And a corporation wants a case that will justify its investment to stockholders.

But organizations don't submit proposals to boards of trustees; people submit proposals to people.

Once the volunteer and the prospective donor are together, the volunteer's own personal influence can count more than anything else. What the volunteer says, and how they say it, will have the greatest impact on the outcome. Ultimately, the best tool of persuasion is the volunteer's own sincerity, interest and enthusiasm.

In other words, once the formalities are taken care of, the volunteer can act as the old saying advises: "Words that come from the heart enter the heart."

John D. Rockefeller, Jr. said it all (it took him a few words, to do it, but they're worth reading):

"When a solicitor comes to you and lays on your heart the responsibility that rests so heavily on his; when his earnestness gives convincing evidence of how seriously interested he is; when he makes it clear that he knows you are no less anxious to do your duty in the matter than he is, that you are just as conscientious, that he feels sure all you need is to realize the importance of the enterprise and the urgency of the need in order to lead you to do your full share in meeting it—he has made you his friend and has brought you to think of giving not as a duty but as a privilege."

When we ask for money, we are friends, not adversaries. We are counselors, not salesmen. It's not a game of predator and prey. We are trying to help the donor do something significant for the community and for society. After all, we're not asking for anything for ourselves.

Unfortunately, many organizations still think of fund-raising as a "hard sell." They train a "sales force" and put them in the field with sales objectives, quotas and sales promotion literature. But major donors—those who have been contributing large sums of money for a long time—will resist, or worse, yawn. They have become hardened to aggressive, manipulative selling.

In this respect, philanthropy has a feature in common with business. People buy from companies, invest in them and work for them because they feel that the enterprise can satisfy their human wants and desires, and because they believe in the *people* who represent the enterprise.

Every day, we're thinking: What do the people—what does the person—want?

27

The Right Person Makes the Difference

WHAT IS THE SECRET of fund-raising success?

Many a veteran will say, "Select the right person to ask the right person, in the right way, for the right amount, for the right reason, at the right time."

This old maxim of fund-raising still holds true, although it's a little mysterious. It's like that sure-fire formula for making a bundle in the stock market: "Only buy stocks that are going up."

Both these pieces of advice point you in the right direction, but don't tell you how to get there. The "how" depends on circumstance and opportunity—the kind of realities that require the judgment of one who is seasoned, usually a professional.

People who are experienced at assessing these situations will usually insist on holding out for the "right person" to call on a certain prospective donor. They know that people are just plain more receptive if they're asked by someone they respect. In practice, this usually means a peer or someone at what seems to be a higher level of influence.

Often, it's not a question of the "right person," but of the "right people"—a team of two working together. As it is written in the Talmud, "If two logs are dry and one is wet, the kindling of the two will kindle the wet one, too."

The sequence in which volunteers see people is important, too. The prospective donor who is seen first is the one considered most likely to come through at the suggested level. The success of this first call can influence both the one who asks and the one who's asked in subsequent calls.

The whole idea is to be *strategic*. The campaign director or the chief development officer, if they are a good listener, is in the best position to be the primary strategist.

28

The One Who Asks First Gives

He: YOU KNOW, you ought to get some of that company's stock. They're really going places.

She: Really? How much did you buy?

He: Oh, I didn't buy any yet. I'm planning to. I just think it's a good idea for you.

In business or in philanthropy, a person's actions are more convincing than their advice. There's nothing wrong with good advice and good intentions, but the force of example is more compelling. In practice, a leader is one who expresses convictions through actions.

This is the cardinal rule of raising money: A volunteer first makes a *personal commitment* before asking others. That is a given.

To be even more effective, the volunteer will want to give at the proper level. That level would be no less, according to the volunteer's means, than what the prospective donor is being invited to do.

As Socrates counseled: "Let him that would move the world first move himself."

29

See Each Person Face to Face

IF WE REALLY BELIEVE that people are more important than dollars, then we owe it to our top prospective donors to visit them in person. Besides, seeing people face to face *works* better than any other method.

In philanthropy, as in friendship, the letter and the telephone can get things started—or keep them going—but the *real* relationship is built in person. Nothing says you care like being there.

The prospective donor is called on the phone only to set up an appointment. The danger is being drawn into soliciting by long distance. If this happens, the person will never know how willing we were to take the time for a personal visit.

The plan for a broad-based campaign may call for inviting smaller gifts by telephone, mail or even television. Even here, the more personal we can get, the better the results will be. We can use the telephone script to provide a framework, but we *listen* to the person. It is a conversation, not a sales pitch. When we write a letter to 10,000 people, it's most effective to write for just *one* person.

The same principle applies when recruiting volunteers: Get as personal as you can. Always enlist a person *in* person.

30

Ask for a Specific Amount; Ask for Enough

MOST PROSPECTIVE DONORS want some guidance—the more specific, the better. "Whatever you can do" is a recipe for failure. It suggests that the organization is ambiguous about the whole enterprise.

Again, John D. Rockefeller, Jr. spoke for most donors:

> "I do like a man to say to me, "We are trying to raise $4 million, and are hoping you may be desirous of giving ___ dollars. If you see your way clear to do so, it will be an enormous help and encouragement. You may have it in mind to give more; if so, we shall be glad. On the other hand, you may feel you cannot give as much, in view of other responsibilities. If that is the case, we shall understand."

Many volunteers are also surprised to learn that prospective donors prefer to be asked for *enough*: enough to reflect their stature and capability, and enough to really get the job done. People, once motivated to contribute, are likely to be embarrassed by a request to give *less* than they're able.

(Please don't follow the example set by a famous neurological institute when they asked their doctors to bequeath their brains for research. They ended their appeal with the traditional line: "Any contribution, however small, will be gratefully appreciated.")

If they're going to be associated with a program, most people genuinely want to make investments that will help to ensure its success. Many donors would agree with the sentiment expressed by a friend many years ago: "Don't give until it hurts. Give until it feels good."

It's easier to "feel good" if we have something against which to measure our performance. That's why specificity—at a level commensurate with a person's financial capacity and their stake in the community—tends to be most effective in raising funds.

31

Qualify the Person

WHAT YOU ASK a particular person to give is based on what they *could* give—if properly motivated and asked by the right person. The key is what the person is capable of, not what you think they likely to do. Rather than saying, "This is what we have you down for," the figure is presented as a suggested guideline—a "think about" figure. It's proportional to what others in similar financial circumstances are being asked to consider.

How do you determine what to ask for?

The best way is to organize a committee of peers—an evaluation committee. This group studies the standards chart (the number of contributions at each level that it will take to reach the goal), and tries to decide which people are capable of investing at these levels.

For the suggested asking figures to be effective, serious thought is given to the membership of this anonymous committee. Certainly, you want people who are aware of people's means. But you'll be a step ahead if you include those who are likely to become part of the program's leadership. They'll be able to defend their evaluations, if need be, and their own sights may well be raised by participating in this process. Research by the development staff, using public record information, can help to fill in the picture.

It's been proven time and again: If the people who will be responsible for asking for money have had a good deal to say about how much will be asked for, from whom and for what, then *their* program has a better chance to succeed.

Of course, in evaluations of prospective donors, confidentiality is the rule. We don't want to infringe on people's privacy. But we do want to use evaluations to make sure that our energies are concentrated on those people who have the capacity to realize our goals. It's unfair to ask a volunteer to "aim high" when making their call without providing this information.

When it comes to corporate and foundation philanthropy, various methods can be brought into play when setting "think about" figures. One medical center, for example, looked at the percentage of the goal that each corporate donor contributed to the last campaign, nine years earlier. (If you use this method, remember that many things can change with time—a corporation's capacity and willingness to give, its priorities, its leadership and its relationships with organizations.)

In a university campaign, another formula was used to establish the figure: a simple $500 per employee. Sales or net income, if they can be learned, may provide more equitable standards. But we want to watch for turning voluntary giving into something that looks like taxation.

Sectors of the corporate community, such as banks or insurance companies, may decide to give a certain percentage of the goal as a group. Many companies relate their giving to what the biggest company in town does, or consult informally with each other during the "think about" period.

—⁓—

Before evaluations begin, there are two other determinations that are made. The first, some say, is to qualify your prospects and separate them from "suspects."

A qualified prospective donor is one who has the *financial capability.* They would have some *rationale* for giving to the program—a philosophical rationale, if not active interest or involvement in the organization. And they would have some *history of giving*—to other organizations, if not to your own. It's very difficult to turn a non-giver into a giver.

A second crucial determination is the *pathway* to the person. Unless someone has access to the individual, they are still what some call a "suspect." In so many communities, the out-of-town consultant is told: "There's a lot of money in this community." The consultant, with good reason, will usually respond: "That's great. Now who's going to go out and ask for it?"

Evaluation is a sensitive and time-consuming process, but an essential one. Those who put in long hours as anonymous members of the evaluation committee are among the unsung heroes of philanthropic success. Without them, few campaigns would succeed.

32

Tenacity Prevails

"LET ME TELL YOU the secret that has led me to my goal," said Louis Pasteur. "My strength lies solely in my tenacity."

The playwright Noel Coward agreed: "Thousands of people have talent. I might as well congratulate you for having eyes in your head. The one and only thing that counts is: Do you have staying power?"

Let's face it: Before a commitment can be secured from a person, a volunteer may easily end up calling on the person two, three or four times. It will almost always take more than one visit to provide the natural "think about" time.

There are a couple of techniques to keep in mind. First, if the person is dubious or hasn't made a decision yet, it's probably unwise to rush them into a premature "no"—or a token gift. It's better to give the person some time to think it over, and give yourself some time to strategize.

You may spend the first visit or two just providing information, answering questions—being a good *investment counselor*. The "order" may not even be asked for until the individual appears ready to place it. Perhaps the volunteer will come back with another to assist, or a new idea to motivate the person—such as a commemorative opportunity or a creative financial vehicle.

Just make sure that before you leave the person, you have a definite appointment to return.

And whatever you do, keep yourself encouraged. Remember, even Babe Ruth struck out 1,330 times.

33

Ask for the Order

WITHOUT THE INVITATION to invest, there would be fewer commitments made.

Everyone experienced in raising money has a personal version of the old story: A major commitment comes from an unexpected source. When the donor is asked why they never gave before, the answer is, "Because nobody ever asked me."

Some donors, of course, prefer to offer, rather than to be asked—especially if "asking" means the old-fashioned "hard sell." Philanthropist Albert Ratner of Cleveland is one:

"I'll kick out of my office anyone who comes and says, 'I've got you down for such-and-such an amount.' Instead, the solicitor should tell me about the program, about the plans and about his interest in them. Then, at the end of the discussion, I will naturally ask him how I can help, how much I can give and what good that amount of money will do."

In philanthropy, clearly, a premature discussion of money is no better than the car salesman telling you the price before showing you the car. But where some of us get off the path is in waiting *too* long.

Words more enduring than these have not been written: "Ask, and it shall be given you; seek, and ye shall find."

A more contemporary sage, Will Rogers, put it this way: "Even if you're on the right track, you'll get run over if you just sit there." We can do our research; we can cultivate their interest, involve them. But if we don't move ahead and invite them, we may have missed our opportunity.

VI

Practicing Stewardship

*This task is not
to get a donation, but
to develop a donor.*

34

The Donor Deserves Good Stewardship

IN BUSINESS, THE OBJECTIVE is not to make a sale, but to make a customer. In philanthropy, the objective is not to secure a donation, but to *develop a donor.*

Our job is not finished when the invitations to invest are completed, the commitments made, and the goal achieved. That's when the task of stewardship *begins.*

Good stewardship means protecting and managing the donor's investment—so that it produces the best possible return. It means using the money as the donor intended it to be used.

The National 4-H Council believes so strongly in this principle that it provides donors with a signed agreement that specifies what the organization will do in exchange for the donor's investment.

Good stewardship also means thanking the contributor. We owe it to donors to recognize their deeds. As Seneca wrote, "There is as much greatness of mind in acknowledging a good turn, as in doing it." Moreover, it's in the organization's own best interest to express its thanks. As it's often said, the first step in attracting the next investment is acknowledging the last.

A "thank you" note is sent on the same day as the contribution is received. But there's a better way than to send a form letter, hang a plaque or issue a bulletin. It's better if a *personal* letter, a *personal* telephone call, a *personal* visit.

And it's even better to express gratitude more than once. "Go often to the house of thy friend," advises an old Scandinavian proverb, "for weeds soon choke up the unused path." Report to the donor the benefits that have come from their investment.

If donors only hear from us when we're asking for money, they'll be less likely to respond. Build ongoing relationships with your contributors. Invite them. Recognize them. Involve them. Ask them. Send them information before others receive it.

———❧———

The principles of good stewardship apply to the way we treat volunteers, as well as donors. The people who raise the money deserve our thanks and recognition. We want to stay in touch with them, to keep them involved. Contrary to popular opinion, leaving someone on the shelf isn't "saving" them for later; we're distancing ourselves from them and letting the relationship slide.

In a way, stewardship begins as soon as a volunteer joins the team. We want to do everything we can to give the volunteer a good experience

If it seems that good stewardship will use up a lot of energy, it will. (It will also generate a lot.) One way to look at it is to consider stewardship a "cost of doing business." One YMCA appropriates a small percentage of the dollars it raises toward this cost.

Good stewardship is well worth the extra effort it requires. It is the bedrock on which the future of an organization is built.

VII

Kindling
the Spirit of
Philanthropy

Inspire the best

people to become your

best advocates.

35

The Best Advocate Is Both Donor and Volunteer

IN THE ART AND SCIENCE of philanthropy, when all is said and done, our mission is this: to inspire the best people to become our best advocates.

The best advocates inspire others by the force of example. The advocate gives and asks others to give, works and asks others to work.

These are four aspects of the same impulse—the philanthropic spirit. In our urge to make fund-raising more specialized, more professional, more sophisticated, we always want to keep in sight this essential and beautiful simplicity.

"What it's all about," says one veteran trustee, "is asking the most respected and successful people: 'if you believe in this cause, as I do, will you make as large an investment in it as you can, and will you ask another to do the same?'"

All the ideas and techniques described in this book spring from this dynamic: inviting others to join together with us in doing important things. Everything we do in the course of raising money, we do to facilitate this process, to help it unfold—for the benefit of the cause, the donor, the community, the nation, yes, even the world.

In the realm of raising money, we are more than mere technicians. Certainly, we're far from going back and being beggars or predators. Our mission is to provide people with opportunities to do great things ... to challenge and inspire them ... to involve them in enterprises that will make life better for our generation, and future generations—enterprises that will advance our civilization as only voluntary action can.

If we can succeed in this quest, our attention will turn from the techniques of raising money. For we will have succeeded in kindling the spirit of philanthropy.

A Word on
Fund-Raising Professionals
and Consultants

Development expertise

is an investment,

rather than an expense.

Hire the Best—and Let Them Direct

TRUSTEES AND THEIR chief executives are well advised to hire the best development professionals they can attract. If they do, the board will be free to focus their energies where they'll be most effective—using their influence with peers, rather than in managing the development program.

It's a simple equation. When the professional's knowledge of development and skills in management are combined with the volunteer's leadership and influence, the result is success.

The development officer, in most cases, is not expected to personally solicit contributions or recruit volunteers. Instead, the development officer is expected to see that these things are done, and done well— at times perhaps accompanying the volunteer who is making the visit.

What makes a good development officer?

- The effective development executive has finely-tuned interpersonal skills. The basic question is: Can they inspire the kind of confidence that will draw people to the program?

  The senior development officer will form close working relationships with the CEO and the board in order to be able to direct their activities in development.

When they become accepted as the insistent voice for the basic principles and techniques of the field, you're well on your way. In most situations, the professional is expected to provide formal training in those principles and techniques for the trustees and volunteers.

- The best development professionals are strategists. Many provide a development plan, including objectives, policies, procedures, organization, timetable and budget. It's not unusual to hear the executive repeat the well-worn phrase: "Plan the work and work the plan."

- The development officer is also a manager and technician—acting as administrator of the development or campaign office and controller of its systems. The solid professional, for example, will ensure that all names are spelled correctly—because experience has taught that in development, small (and very important) details and grand design must come together.

———

Before you can build or expand a development office, however, the perennial question of cost presents itself. There's a good deal of truth in the old bromide, "You've got to spend money to raise money." The costs of a development operation can be an investment, rather than an expense item. If you plan well, the returns will tend to be proportionate to the "front-end" investment.

"It is unwise to pay too much, but worse to pay too little," said John Ruskin. "When you pay too little, you sometimes lose all, because the thing you bought was incapable of doing the thing it was bought to do."

"The common law of business balance prohibits paying little and getting a lot," Ruskin warned. "It can't be done."

In a sense, the development function is like any business operation. The greatest risk for either enterprise is in the early years, when they are most vulnerable to the effects of undercapitalization.

Money, however, is not the only way to attract talented staff members. They want to work for an organization that has the potential for achievement. It's true that for most professionals, one symbol of the organization's commitment is its front-end investment in the program. Another is its willingness to provide the time over which to build a strong program.

It's not uncommon, for example, for a new annual giving program to "lose money" for a couple of years. In planned giving, it may take longer to bring a commitment to a close. Even more time may be required to get the organization ready to launch a successful capital campaign.

This, of course, is just another way of pointing up the value of "up-front" investment. If time is not provided, the development process will degenerate into a series of "shakedowns"—in which the easy money is taken, and the building of relationships neglected.

There are, unfortunately, some professionals who will use a "grace period" to lose themselves in the process—never to be seen again. These nomads move to another organization after a year or two, repeating their act. Fortunately, they are few in number.

In sum, the best development professional is an effective planner, strategist, director, facilitator, communicator and administrator.

Some would say that these terms describe any competent manager in today's business world. That's probably true; for this job description has been modeled for us, to a great extent, by the development officers who are in business—the outside fund-raising consultants who are discussed on the following pages.

Counsel Can Help to Ensure Success

ONCE AN ORGANIZATION has "gone public" with its plans for development, the community's leadership will be watching closely to see what happens. For them, success in the familiar area of raising money is more visible than the work of even the most well-run outfit.

On the other hand, a program that flounders and falls short of its goal can be a terrible setback to the reputation of any organization. Contributions and volunteers will be harder to come by the next time— which may be a long way off.

Because the outcome is so crucial, many organizations take out an "insurance policy" by engaging professional fund-raising counsel.

While they offer many other benefits, chief may be sheer measurable results. The best firms are known for making the goal. After all, their reputations—and their survival as businesses—depend on it. They may even be able to "create" a campaign where one didn't seem possible.

Fund-raising consultants are available in various specialties: direct mail, planned giving and the like. This discussion focuses on those who consult on campaigns and ongoing development programs.

These consultants fall into two categories. Some provide periodic services and act primarily as advisors. Others provide on-site direction of a program, usually on a full-time basis.

The consultant who acts only as an advisor may provide service at a lower total cost. They may even offer a more advanced approach. A consultant, however, cannot manage volunteers and staff as well as an on-site director.

The solution? Today, many firms provide periodic consultation before the campaign; then full-time, resident direction during the intensive period. Finally, periodic consultation is made available after the campaign.

—◦◦◦—

What are the advantages of retaining counsel? Here are the major ones.

First is independence. Counsel's autonomy can make it easier for them to say what's important to say, and to insist on doing things right.

Because counsel has gained objectivity through many different experiences, it can be easier for them to interpret and analyze many situations and to recommend the best course of action. Counsel that is trusted is also in a position to learn things that might not be shared so candidly with someone closer to the organization.

For these reasons, many veteran fund-raisers believe that outside counsel is just about the only agency that can conduct an effective feasibility study.

Another advantage is that counsel can provide the sheer manpower (or, today, womanpower) to do the full-time job of directing a campaign—and do it without diversion. Counsel's ability to provide a concentrated effort also lends a sense of urgency to the enterprise that springs from all of the forward motion that can be generated and their "running meter," rather than the "needs" of the organization.

Counsel can be valuable for any number of other reasons. For example, because they've done it before, they can estimate with a measure of accuracy how much a given program will cost, and how long it will take.

Counseling firms charge for their services on a fee basis, in the same way as legal and accounting firms.

Most respectable firms will charge a fixed fee, whether the effort exceeds its goal or falls short.

———

Much of what can be said for the better firms or solo practitioners can also be said for the experienced in-house professional. The development expert, whether with a consulting firm or on the organization's staff, knows what is vital to be done and what is superfluous.

Beware of the professional who agrees with you on everything. Either they're less than honest or they're duplicating your own efforts. As William Wrigley used to say, "When two people agree all the time, one of them is unnecessary."

I've been through the process of selecting counsel and echo others who often offer this advice: Beware of the slick sales presentation that provides an easy answer to every difficult question. Instead, look for evidence that the firm has listened to you—and wants to design a program for your specific situation, while staying true to what their experiences have taught them.

One last advantage of working with counsel: They are part of the business community, and as such, are likely to have a keen sense of the values and concerns of donors. I'll never forget Carlton Ketchum's early edict to his campaign directors: "Always wear a hat and never smoke a cigar. "

Afterword

How raising money

can be one of the most

important and rewarding steps

you'll take this year.

IF YOU WERE TO TAKE just one idea from this book, I would want it to be this: People want to give. They want to invest themselves in the future.

As simple as that sounds, everything changes when we truly believe it.

Yet these same folks who want to give often carry a question in the back of their minds: "Can I really make a difference?"

That's when we arrive in the picture. You and I come along and open a conversation. In time, we invite a deed of philanthropy.

Our simple act of showing up gives the donor a reason to believe that one person can indeed take initiative and make a difference. For we've made the effort to come to them. And we've made a difference by making our own commitment. We are an example in their life of personal initiative in action.

Hope

OUR PRESENCE BOLSTERS their confidence in the future, especially if we walk in with more hope than needs.

Often that's all it takes, just someone giving voice to (even legitimizing) hope and confidence, to change their corner of the world and the wider world they influence.

That hope feeds civic and philanthropic behavior.

Heroism

IN A TIME THAT CALLS for deeds of optimistic courage in our voluntary sector and in society as a whole, you and I get to give people an opportunity to come to terms with their own heroism. They may even discover within themselves more than they ever imagined was there.

In this stepping out, they become heroic. To call it anything less is to do a disservice to their role, for it undervalues the courage it takes to make a significant philanthropic investment, and the leadership it provides.

If they come to be seen as heroic, then you the hero-maker. That just might be a more essential role, even more of a heroic journey.

What Kind of World Do You Want?

YOU HAVE ASSOCIATED yourself with a cause larger than any one person. In making your own commitment you have taken a stand for hope and courage.

You now have the privilege to invite others to do the same. Their act will be a declaration of what's important to them and give tangible evidence of the kind of person they are, the influence they want to have in the world.

Given this, how strange it sounds if the operative question is the usual one: "What does the organization need, and how can we get the money for it?"

Instead, how much better when it becomes: "What kind of world does each of us want, and how can we realize that future?"

Acknowledgments

THE GREATEST INSPIRATION for this book was provided by the volunteers and the donors with whom I have been privileged to work—people like Joseph B. Dahlkemper of Erie, Pennsylvania.

Once, when I asked him why he thought philanthropy was important, Mr. Dahlkemper paused for a moment, looked into the distance and began to speak from the heart:

> My grandparents were farmers. When I was a child, I asked them why they sometimes turned crops back into the soil, instead of harvesting them. They told me that the earth had been good to them, and if they wanted it to continue to be productive, they needed to return something to the ground. Isn't that what we're doing in our community? Isn't that why philanthropy makes so much sense?

Behind these volunteers are the professionals who manage development programs.

Among the others to whom a debt is owed:

Harold J. "Si" Seymour—who made a lasting contribution to the literature of the field with his still-quoted *Designs for Fund Raising* and other occasional papers, which provided me with much inspiration.

R. Blair Schreyer, president of Ketchum, Inc. and past chairman of the American Association of Fund-Raising Counsel—who first delivered me into the world of capital campaigns.

Derek VanPelt—who, as my editor on the first edition, helped me understand what I was trying to say. His friendship, and his knowledge of development and marketing, have been most valuable.

My wife, Wendy—who gave the sustenance that allowed the inspiration to be committed to paper.

And the Ben Kaufmans of this world.

And a special note added to the second edition to acknowledge the single person who contributed the most to bringing this book to its hard-to-believe level of popularity. Greg Branstetter's leadership, management and marketing acumen made all the difference. And the single person who brought to life this second edition with her talent in writing and knowing how to bring this book anew to the world—Pam McAllister.

To all these; to the many others who have invested their time in reading the manuscript and providing advice and ideas; and to the thousands who have labored through this material with me as I tested it in speeches, seminars and workshops—I say, "Thank you for the benefit of your talents."

About the Author

JIM LORD HAS DEVOTED his life to expanding what's possible for people who want to change the world. His early work on dozens of capital campaigns gave him a solid grounding in the best conventional practices of raising money and led to the book you hold in your hands. Billions of dollars have been contributed to causes where Jim has served as "thinking partner," with untold more lives influenced and dollars raised by readers of this book for trustees (a book that became the all-time bestselling work in the field, thanks to an amazing number of copies sold in its first decade).

Ever curious about what draws people to pour their hearts and souls into making the world a better place, Jim withdrew from public view and turned his attention to wide-ranging studies of social psychology, personal and organization development, spiritual traditions; indeed, just about every discipline of human knowledge. He put that learning to work in select organizations and communities, developing and testing new methods that bring out the best in people and inspire them to reach for new possibilities.

Decades of learning, experience, and reflection came together in his by-invitation "Philanthropic

Quest" workshops, sought after by leaders of organizations of social good, the philanthropic community, and civic and business leaders from more than 50 countries … and in his forthcoming book: *What Kind of World Do You Want?*

A gift for you, with my thanks

IF THE CONFIDENT stance in these pages resonates with you, I'd like to put even more wind in your sails. After all, you deserve to have all you can have going for you, to make the most of these unusual days.

So I've put together a series of resources designed to take you to your next level of success in influencing— even inspiring—people to get involved, to invest their time and money in what matters.

These are available to you with my compliments, as my way of thanking you for all you're doing … as you invest yourself in your community, and even in the world.

To gain access to these resources, simply send an email to jim@whatkindofworld.com or call my recorded message line any time of day: (206) 527-7408.

Best regards,
Jim Lord

LaVergne, TN USA
30 December 2009
168522LV00001B/4/P

9 780979 948503